I Come Preaching

*The Preacher and His Preaching
from 1 Corinthians*

PAUL
SCHWANKE

First published by Paul Schwanke, an Independent Baptist
evangelist from Lakeside Baptist Church of Peoria, Arizona.
Evangelist Schwanke is committed to preaching
and providing materials to assist pastors and churches
in the fulfillment of the Great Commission.

Evangelist Paul Schwanke
www.preachthebible.com

Cover design by Mr. Rick Lopez
Cover art by Mr. Paul Dykman - *"Standing on Mars Hill"*
Special thanks to Pastors Ken Brooks and J.C. Joiner

ISBN-13: 978-1495218262
ISBN-10: 1495218260

Printed in the United States of America

CONTENTS

PREFACE

APRIL 7, 1984 WAS a beautiful Saturday afternoon in Arcola, Louisiana. Surely you have heard of Arcola, Louisiana. It is after all a suburb of Roseland, which is a suburb of Amite, which is the home of the world famous Amite Oyster Festival. It would be the only place to find a Walmart between Hammond, Louisiana and McComb, Mississippi.

Nine months earlier, I had preached my first meeting as a young evangelist in Connecticut. Getting a start in evangelism is incredibly hard, but the Lord was opening doors for us. Most of them were in the northeast where I had grown up, with people I was accustomed to.

We arrived in 'town' driving our overloaded, lime-green Chevrolet pickup truck, which towed our overloaded 35-foot travel trailer. Somehow, my pregnant wife Cathy and I fit in that single bench along with two little children, who were both in car seats, a feat that took more than a little engineering. We pulled into the parking lot of First Baptist Church of Arcola to start a revival meeting the next day.

That's where I got to know Doctor Bob Simpson.

I had never met anyone quite like Brother Bob before. In all honesty, I have never met anyone quite like Brother Bob since. You see, there are not a lot of Bob Simpsons in Connecticut.

The first thing he did that day was scare me to death. He asked what we were doing there. When I told him we had come for the Revival meeting, he told me it was the wrong week. He pulled my string for a while, and then bellowed a big ole' country laugh. For the rest of the week there were a lot of 'Yankee' jokes, wonderful southern cooking, and special fellowship that changed my life. When we drove off the property a week later, I was a different preacher because of Bob Simpson.

Everything they taught us to do in school, it seemed Brother Bob didn't do. Everything they taught us not to do, it seemed he did. But I learned that week that a man of God walking with God is more concerned about pleasing God than following a human roadmap. I learned that a man might have a different background than I have. He may have gone to a different school. He may have a different accent (though Brother Simpson is quite sure I am the one with the accent). But when he stands up in God's pulpit, he loves the same Savior that I love, and he preaches the same Bible I preach.

I am a man with decades of debt to preachers like Bob Simpson. I have laughed with them, cried with them, listened to them, been taught by them, prayed with them, and discussed preaching with them. From Houlton, Maine; to Ka Lae, Hawaii; from Everett, Washington; to Margate, Florida; with missionaries and pastors on six continents, I have been privileged to stand with wonderful men of God. It is to them and for them this book is written.

The principles and convictions come from 1 Corinthians. The practice has been on display in front of my eyes for more than 30 years.

To Brother Simpson and hundreds like him, I only hope this book serves as a small measure of thanks.

Chapter One
I Come Preaching!

"And my speech and my preaching was not with enticing words of
man's wisdom, but in demonstration of the Spirit and of power:"
1 Corinthians 2:4

WHAT A TRIP it must have been. As the crow flies, the distance between Athens and Corinth was 44 miles. As the human walks, it would take the average man two long days to make the journey.

It is noted that Paul seemed to make that trip alone (Acts 18:1). On most occasions, for safety reasons and spiritual reasons, Paul would travel with an entourage. Usually, it was "they" who journeyed on, but this time, there was no Silas, no Timothy, and no Doctor Luke. It was Paul and his Lord.

Sometimes it is good to wake up in the morning, put on a jacket, and take a long walk as the sun is rising. Perhaps a preacher needs to get in the car and find a country road that doesn't seem to end. It might be an empty beach, a quiet hillside, or a mountain path where a man and his Savior take a walk. It is at those times when He teaches great lessons.

Humanly speaking, Athens would have to be considered a great success. The story could fill a missionary prayer letter, blessing the preacher brethren and encouraging the givers at Antioch, Jerusalem, and points beyond. His disputing with the Jews, the devout persons, the Epicureans, and the Stoicks had so piqued their interest that he was actually invited to the Areopagus (Mars' Hill), where he would address the intellectual elitists in the world capital of philosophy. What an honor!

Mars' Hill is a huge rock that stands under the Acropolis, the home of Greek idols and ancient religion. Even though they are but ruins today, it takes little imagination to visualize Paul standing before the teachers and their temples, moved by their superstitions and ignorance. He would set them straight! He would preach to them a message like they had never heard!

There are many dangers preachers face. Most of them are transparent enough, but often the greatest risks are the ones hardest to recognize. Paul would face sticks and stones and shipwrecks, yet in Athens, he encountered a most powerful foe. It sounded like this:

"What will this babbler say" (Acts 17:18)?

The ridiculing experts were mocking him. The professional skeptics were doubting him. Jesus? The resurrection? This new doctrine had to be explained to the satisfaction of their erudite ears. Their lives were spent in "nothing else, but either to tell, or to hear some new thing" (Acts 17:21).

There was a pressure on Paul that God's preachers must deal with - a pressure that wants to be accepted by this world. Oh, we know the commands. "Be not conformed to this world" (Romans 12:2); "Love not the world" (1 John

2:15); "Friendship of the world is enmity with God" (James 4:4). We hold convictions as Independent Baptists that are not for sale. We know about the Balaams of the world and their propensity to sell out. Not us!

But everyone wants acceptance. No one wants to be mocked by the elitist seminary professor. We do not want to become the fodder for a liberal newspaper journalist or the object of a reporter's exposé. It becomes an easy thing to soften a position, to skip a verse that might offend, or to ignore a message that might be ridiculed by the critics.

So this student of Gamaliel gave them an earful. Paul stood in the "midst of Mars' Hill" and proceeded to stagger them with a discourse lasting for eleven verses that was unlike anything they had ever heard. He expounded of Creation, of the nations, of the Godhead, and of the Resurrection. He was a brilliant man delivering a brilliant discourse. Mars' Hill had met its match! Our guy was better than their guy! We won the debate!

But he never mentioned the Cross. The old 'slaughter-house religion' was a little too coarse a subject for a place like Mars' Hill. Somehow, Calvary didn't seem to fit the setting.

So now he is leaving Athens. He impressed them. He amazed them. He debated them. He 'wowed' them.

But the Savior didn't say, "Impress them. Amaze them. Debate them. Wow them." He said, "Win them. Baptize them. Teach them. Start churches." That cannot be accomplished without preaching the Cross. When Paul departed Athens, he left no church behind.

Ahead is that long, lonely walk to Corinth and, I suspect, a Savior convicting him every step of the way. Perhaps he is crossing the Corinthian Isthmus at the Diolkos, a narrow bridge over the waters, where Paul determines that Athens will never be repeated as long as God gives him breath.

"And I, brethren, when I came to you, came not with excellency of speech or of wisdom, declaring unto you the testimony of God. For I determined not to know any thing among you, save Jesus Christ, and him crucified. And I was with you in weakness, and in fear, and in much trembling. And my speech and my preaching was not with enticing words of man's wisdom, but in demonstration of the Spirit and of power: That your faith should not stand in the wisdom of men, but in the power of God" (2 Corinthians 2:1-5).

We can hear him say, "I am not coming to impress. I am not coming to be liked. I am not coming to be accepted."

"I am coming to preach!"

Chapter Two
The Positive Preacher

"I thank my God always on your behalf..."
1 Corinthians 1:4

THE CORINTHIAN CHURCH was in desperate need of preaching. Every chapter seems to open one more sore, one more conflict in need of healing, troubles the church members often did not recognize.

The church was full of members that considered themselves spiritual giants. How fortunate was Paul to have them for advice! Their great "knowledge" would gladly be imparted to the masses, and their wisdom was the antidote to baby Christianity and its problems. When looking in the spiritual mirror, they were quite awed with what they saw.

Paul, however, was not so impressed. In plain language, he would boldly tell them the truth. "And I, brethren, could not speak unto you as unto spiritual, but as unto carnal, even as unto babes in Christ" (1 Corinthians 3:1). If that wasn't enough, he would tell them their vast storehouse of knowledge only succeeded in puffing them up (1 Corinthians 8:1).

So much for "knowledge."

When the list of Corinthian failures is published, it is not a pretty thing. There was rampant carnality. There was the matter of fornication so base even the pagans wouldn't go there. They were taking the brothers to court over petty matters. There was a faction convinced their "liberty" was more important than the testimony of Christ. And speaking of 'factions,' nobody did it quite like the Corinthian church. The word "divide" and its forms are found repeatedly in the book and for good reason.

When American hunters of past centuries feared an encounter with the brown bear, they would make sure they carried their most powerful weapons, guns unnecessary for smaller game. On such occasions, the hunter would prepare himself for a violent encounter, and it was said that he was 'loaded for bear.'

Paul was 'loaded for bear.' He had 16 chapters worth of material, with a second epistle not far behind. It appears there was at least one other letter trying to fix the mess called the Church of God at Corinth. The man of God was about to unload.

Yet, there is a significant lesson for a preacher in 1 Corinthians 1. In the midst of the disaster, Paul found a way to be positive, something to rejoice in.

We have all heard the story of the man about to jump off a bridge and end it all. The police officer begged him to wait. "Give me ten minutes! Just ten minutes! Talk to me!" The jumper agreed, so he and the officer talked. Ten minutes later, they both jumped off the bridge.

As an evangelist, I know the feeling. Occasionally, I have flown into an airport to preach a revival meeting. The pastor drives up, I toss the bags into the trunk, shake his hand, and then it starts. We are not off the airport property, yet the torrent of church trials and tribulations erupts. There have been meetings where the downpour doesn't stop until I am back at the airport.

It really is hard for a church to be positive when the pastor is negative.

Paul was a great example of a positive preacher. Though it seems the human tendency is to head to the negative, Paul found a better way.

Paul looked for things to be thankful for. He went there first. "I thank my God always on your behalf, for the grace of God which is given you by Jesus Christ" (1 Corinthians 1:4). There are obvious motives for the letter, yet an honest Paul wanted to find reasons to rejoice. Negative people are always looking for something to complain about. Positive people are always looking for things to be thankful for. We will ultimately find what we are looking for.

Paul was thankful for their enrichment. The church at Corinth was a very large church by New Testament standards (some 100 members). Later, we discover that some were wealthy and some were not, but Paul understood that they were all rich. "That in every thing ye are enriched by him, in all utterance, and in all knowledge" (1 Corinthians 1:5). God made them rich in utterance, an ability to speak powerfully. God made them rich in knowledge, an ability critically important in such a city. It was a personal blessing to Paul when he realized that God had empowered and equipped them for the work.

Paul was thankful for the "testimony of Christ" confirmed in them (1 Corinthians 1:6). That testimony was so special they came behind no one - they were 'second to none.' There was a lot to be encouraged about! Everything necessary for victory was already there! With the return of Christ in focus, Paul saw the opportunity to fortify them for the battle. He believed they could change. He believed that God could and would work in their lives, so that despite the issues, they would be "blameless" when they stood at the Judgment Seat of Christ.

Like never before, God's preachers are facing enemies without and within. It may seem as if the war is lost and hope is gone, but Paul had it right. "God is faithful!" (1 Corinthians 1:9). He was faithful when the wheels were coming off in Corinth, and He is faithful today. When friends have disappointed us, when a church has let us down, when financial pressures seem insurmountable, there is someone that never fails.

"God is faithful!"

That is something to be positive about!

Chapter Three
Where Did They Learn That?

*"Now I beseech you...that ye all speak the same thing,
and that there be no divisions among you;"*
1 Corinthians 1:10

THE CHURCH OF GOD AT CORINTH was in the process of being ripped apart by "divisions." Those factions and cracks in the assembly were "among" them (1 Corinthians 1:10), indicating the conflicts originated from within. Often, Paul warned about the enemy without seeking to enter in and thrash the flock, but this was not the case at Corinth. Those little foxes spoiling the vines may have been racial divisions, political divisions, or societal divisions, but the quiet ideologies were bubbling to the surface.

There was also a problem with "contentions" (1 Corinthians 1:11). These were angry, hot disputes that burned out of control, which in turn led to rivalries and verbal war. The word for "contentions" referred to a Greek deity called Eris, who was the goddess of war.

It would seem they had a problem with gossips and cliques. Too bad they couldn't wait a few thousand years so they could 'post' their information on forums and blogs that would enable the church members to pray more potently. They must have had some blowout church business meetings.

I wonder where those carnal church members learned how to do that?

It would seem the church had a few stubborn folks as well. It was the intent of God that they be "perfectly joined together in the same mind and in the same judgment." The scrupulous, spiritual surgeon known as the Lord Jesus wanted to wheel them into the operating room and set their broken spiritual bones (the meaning of the words 'joined together'), so they might think the same way and discern the same way. Their pride wouldn't allow it.

I wonder where those carnal church members learned how to do that?

Their battles weren't so private. The whole family of Chloe knew the story and exposed it to Paul. We are not sure where the family of Chloe came from, but it is very possible they were from another city such as Ephesus. Later, their conflicts were said to be "reported commonly" (1 Corinthians 5:1). Their squabbles had moved from the conference room to the front page of the 'Corinth Times.'

I wonder where those carnal church members learned how to do that?

It went from bad to worse. These people actually created 'camps.' There was the 'Paul Camp,' the 'Apollos Camp,' the 'Cephas (Peter) Camp,' and the 'Christ Camp.' Who would ever have thought?

As the camp that followed the official father of the church, the 'Paul Camp' hearkened back to the good ole' days. Paul had been gone for a number of years, but that never seems to stop the 'that's the way we have always done it' crowd.

Apollos was an eloquent Egyptian, mighty in the Scriptures (Acts 18:24). His home city of Alexandria hosted the most respected universities of the Mediterranean, and as such was renowned as the home of scholarship and intelligentsia. The 'Apollos Camp' may well have been a group that revered scholarship and their favorite school.

There is no Bible evidence that Peter ever came to Corinth, but that was no reason to stop the 'Peter Camp.' This faction may have been dispersed Jews who settled in Corinth, people who were more interested in making the church a carbon copy of their predominately Jewish church in Jerusalem. They had their own set of rules and standards that were beyond the Bible, but woe to the man that did not see it their way.

Last, but assuredly not least, (especially in their own minds), was the 'Christ Camp.' Though they had the most spiritual name, their thinking may have been responsible for the rise of the false doctrine called Gnosticism which would plague local churches for decades. When they boasted, "We are of Christ," they were implying that everyone who did not see things their way was not of Christ. They were not just the true believers, they were the only believers.

Amazing! Camps!

I wonder where those carnal church members learned how to do that?

As they were debating over their spiritual credentials bestowed on them when Paul was lowering some of them into the waters of baptism, they had forgotten something more important. They were so busy battling, they forgot that they were supposed to be preaching "the Gospel" (1 Corinthians 1:17), seeing converts baptized, teaching the whole counsel of God, and starting churches. They were so worried about their petty, tiny issues that they had forgotten why they were really there.

I wonder where those carnal church members learned how to do that?

Chapter Four
Sent to Preach

"For Christ sent me..."
1 Corinthians 1:17

WHAT A MISSION field. Nearly a quarter of a million people were squeezed into the metropolis of Corinth, making it the largest city Paul had yet encountered. Surrounded by two harbors, it was a world class trading center. There were citizens of immense wealth yet multitudes of slaves working the ports. We would call the church at Corinth an 'inner city church'.

Corinth was opulent, perhaps the most dazzling of Greek cities. Success in the business world brought an arrogance that infected even the local church. Paul would have to condemn what he called the "spirit of this world," (1 Corinthians 2:12) an attitude that stifled the work of God.

Corinth was a religious city. At least 16 different gods have been identified that were deified in that day. They claimed to magnify all gods, and Rome would let it go so long as there was no hindrance to the government. Christians were branded as enemies because they refused to bow the knee. When they would not participate in the religious feasts, they were viewed as divisive and troublesome.

Corinth was a wicked city. Their reputation was so perverse, the Greeks ultimately coined the word 'corinthian' to mean one who led a life of debauchery. Dominating the city was a hill some 1850 feet high called the 'Acrocorinth,' where stood a large temple to the Greek goddess of love, Aphrodite. The 1,000 priestesses of the temple, known as 'sacred' prostitutes, came down into the city when evening fell and plied their trade in the streets.[1] The city glorified immorality.

What an overwhelming place to start a church!

We have all heard of preachers looking over their city and being moved by the sheer numbers of the population. We lift up our eyes, look on the fields, and we are overcome by the immensity of it all. I recently preached in Shanghai, China, an enormous city of nearly 25 million people. I met with a pastor serving in Beijing, another city of more than 20 million people. Our next stop was in Kunming, a relatively small city in China with 'only' 6½ million souls.

Talk to a missionary in Mexico City, Seoul, or Tokyo, and it won't take long before the burdens and frustrations of attempting to reach untold millions pour out of their hearts. The white harvest fields fill us with a desperate recognition of our own inadequacies.

The human tendency calls for a new plan, a new idea, a new strategy. They certainly have their place, but it is also critical we never lose our purpose. A good coach knows the best way to break a losing streak is to get back to fundamentals. A military leader understands the importance of clear, crisp orders.

When Paul was overwhelmed, he reminded himself why he had come to Corinth. It sounded like this:

"For Christ sent me not to baptize, but to preach the gospel: not with wisdom of words, lest the cross of Christ should be made of none effect" (1 Corinthians 1:17).

When an element in the church thought their baptizer made them greater, it was time to get back to the bottom line. Paul put the focus back to the Cross, reminding them that the Christian life was all about the Savior and His salvation. When they were bickering, Paul went back to square one.

I am sent "to preach".

He went on to offer advice that he lived by, a perfect wisdom for all Bible preachers to follow:

First, never forget that you are sent. Paul was sent out on a mission to establish churches around the world. There was a point in time on the road to Damascus when Jesus saved him and he surrendered his will. There was a point in time God put him "into the ministry". (1 Timothy 1:12)

It is wise to go back to that point. The ministry has a way of getting very complicated, yet it is critical we remind ourselves this is not a profession or a job. This is a calling. We have been sent by Christ.

Secondly, we have one person to please. Paul acknowledged the danger of preaching with the "wisdom of words". In a city like Corinth, a sophisticated homily with lofty words would receive great praise from people. It might be a good speech, but we must remember that preaching is not a good speech!

At the end of the day, the critics in Corinth said his speaking ability was "contemptible" (2 Corinthians 10:10). Paul responded with a 'so what!' He was not there to impress them or receive their praise, nor did he desire their honorary degree. As he was sent by Christ, he was called to preach Christ, and he only cared to please Christ. What a critical reminder for us.

Thirdly, if Christ is exalted, I have done my job. When there is an impressive array of human thinking and philosophy, a preacher leaves the pulpit feeling good about himself. He has stimulated the masses, and they leave the service regaling his ability. But he has made the cross of "none effect". It is impossible to exalt a preacher and a Savior. It is one or the other. Either He will increase and I will decrease, or I will increase and he will decrease. There is room for one on the throne, and if we set ourselves there, no place is left for Him.

Someone once told John Bunyan he had preached a delightful sermon. "You are too late," said the preacher. "The devil told me that before I left the pulpit." [2]

When the burden is great, and the load seems too heavy, it is time to get back to basics.

I am sent "to preach".

Chapter Five
Foolishness!

*"For the preaching of the cross is to them that perish foolishness;
but unto us which are saved it is the power of God."*
1 Corinthians 1:18

IN THE EARLY 1900's, George Bennard traveled for the Salvation Army. He loved to dwell on John 3:16, and he said the more he would quote it, the more alive and powerful it became. He did not picture a gold-colored cross one might hang around a neck but a rough and rugged one, stained with the blood of God's son. A melody came quickly, but the only words that came to him said, "I'll cherish the old rugged cross." For months, he was unable to add to those words.

At a revival meeting in New York, he was impressed of God to preach nightly on the Cross. Multitudes trusted the Lord, claiming the finished work of the Savior as their only hope. So moved by the message of Calvary in his own soul, George Bennard returned home to Michigan, sat down at his kitchen table, and wrote the rest of the beloved song.[3]

We honor the cross, we magnify the cross, and we cherish the cross. Like Paul of old, we have invested our lives, our fortunes, our all in the "preaching of the cross" (1 Corinthians 1:18).

But the world sees it differently. They look at the bloody cross of Calvary and call it "foolishness". Foolishness! No wonder we can't find middle ground with them. We are on polar ends of the spectrum. Calvary is everything to us. Calvary is nothing to them. Calvary is our hope. Calvary is their curse. We sing of Calvary. They laugh at Calvary.

When Paul came preaching the Cross in the city of Corinth, he was met with the same derision found today in the liberal seminary classrooms. Centuries of religion have softened the meaning of the Cross, but in Paul's day such preaching was repulsive. When the people called it "foolishness," they were claiming the message to be absurd. It was folly to the lost man, but Paul did not come to impress the lost man. He came to exalt His Savior.

Paul was coming to preach the Cross. To the unsaved Corinthians, there were reasons such a message was foolish:

Preaching the Cross was an offensive message. It is interesting to note that Paul did not come preaching the resurrection but rather the cross. It was a message about rejection. Jesus was rejected by the multitude, by the religious establishment, by the government, and by His own disciples. It would be a message rejected by most in Corinth.

Preaching the Cross was a confusing message. In our day, we are used to seeing the cross as a symbol, but in the first century it was not so. Cicero, the famous Roman philosopher, exclaimed, "The very word 'cross' should be far removed not only from the person of a Roman citizen but from his thoughts, his eyes and his ears."[4] To preach a crucified Jew as being the divine Son of God and then saving the world by a cross was considered a message of madness.

Preaching the Cross was a repulsive message. There is no glory, no beauty, no attraction in a cross. Religion attracts people to its shrines with majestic art, impressive statutes, stately procession, and glorious music, yet none of those things was central in the Bible. To make the cross a centerpiece of a religion in the days of Paul would be like making an electric chair the focal point of a new religion today.

Preaching the Cross was a powerless message. To the Greeks, the story of Calvary would have seemed an incredible waste. They wanted to hear of a noble hero dying in a magnanimous effort to save his nation, someone who would conquer the enemies of the state. He could not die on a cross like a runaway slave or a common criminal. It would have been tempting for a lesser preacher to reshape Jesus into a Greek champion of sorts, but Paul would have none of that. Without apology, he was coming to preach the cross, and if the world of Corinth thought that foolish, so be it.

Today, we face a similar temptation. We are aware of the liberal denominations that have removed 'bloody songs' from their hymnal. We know of the false prophets that despise the 'slaughter-house religion', deriding the precious blood. We cannot allow them to embarrass us into silence about the Cross.

We cannot place an emphasis anywhere but the Cross. It may be the world wants self-help philosophies, self-esteem and its psychologies, soft messages that tickle the ears, but God did not call us to give people what they want. He called us to preach the Cross!

When the evangelist Billy Sunday was waxing bold about the blood of Christ, a more refined minister wondered aloud if the message should be toned down. "After all, Mr. Sunday, aren't you afraid that you are going to rub the fur the wrong way?" The reply was classic Billy Sunday: "The old cat's heading toward Hell. If she'll turn around, I will rub her the right way."[5]

The Cross was not popular then, and it is not popular now. It was foolish to the lost Corinthian then, it is foolish to the lost man today. It was an object of ridicule then; it is an object of ridicule now. We are not called to have men like us, to be popular, nor to gain the approval of the world.

We are called to preach the Cross.

Chapter Six

Powerful!

"For the preaching of the cross is to them that perish foolishness;
but unto us which are saved it is the power of God."
1 Corinthians 1:18

THE ROMAN WORLD lusted for power. It wasn't simply
the rulers and kings and emperors thirsting to rule the
world, it was the little guy too. Power was everything.

There is a special power in preaching the Cross, a
power the unsaved world cannot begin to comprehend.
When Paul was preaching, the Corinthians were either
shaking their heads in disbelief or rolling on the ground in
derision. The famous first century 'Alexamenos graffito' in
Rome portrays their mockery of the Cross, exhibiting a
man on a cross with the head of a donkey, and an
inscription telling a young man to worship his god.[6]

Power? If He was so powerful, why did He die on a
cross? Did not power go to the conquerors and not the
conquered? How can victory come from death? How can
someone so humbled be so exalted? If the cross is a picture
of evil, shame, rejection, and punishment, how can
anything convincing be associated with it?

The paradoxes are endless. Hebrews 12:3 calls it the
"contradiction of sinners," and those "contradictions" did

not simply puzzle the ancient Corinthians, they confuse modern day Corinthians. Yet, a saved man understands. To him, the preaching of the Cross is "the power of God" (1 Corinthians 1:18). It is the dynamite that disintegrates the shackles of sin controlling a life, the explosion in the soul that delivers a man from the bondage of religion. It is used of God to transform a man, to make a child of God out of a child of Satan, and to replace Hell with Heaven.

When reading verse 18, the expected parallel does not emerge. It would seem to the logician that the verse should read like this: "For the preaching of the cross is to them that perish foolishness; but unto us which are saved it is the (*wisdom*) of God." Wisdom is the opposite of foolishness, but God had a stronger point to make.

The preaching of the Cross is the *power of God*. It is not a symbol of the power of God. It is not a demonstration of the power of God. It is the power God. Romans 1:16 states, "For I am not ashamed of the gospel of Christ: for it is the power of God unto salvation to every one that believeth; to the Jew first, and also to the Greek."

Preaching the Cross must be singular preaching. Note that the Gospel is "the" power of God to save. It is not a critical component of Salvation. It is the only way to be saved.

A missionary in Africa led a religious young man to Christ. A few days later, he ran into the young man and could not help but notice the broad smile on his face. He said, "You certainly look different!" The reply, "I used to think that Jesus was necessary. Now I know that Jesus is enough!"

Exactly right. He is enough!

Preaching the Cross must be hopeful preaching. The Cross is "the power of God unto salvation". For a world bound in sin, He alone has the power to set a man free. He died so I can live; He suffered so I can be free; He was punished so I can receive mercy. There is no case too hard, no sinner gone too far, where the grace of Calvary cannot reach him.

When I was preaching in Papua New Guinea, a woman responded to the invitation to receive Christ. Her husband had been a notorious thief, arrested and jailed many times. Three sons, each following the footsteps of their dad, had been shot and killed by the police. A persistent pastor would not quit praying for and working with the man, and one day, he was saved.

His wife was so amazed by the change in his life, she finally had to come to Christ. It wasn't a persuasive message that grabbed her heart, it was the dynamite of the Gospel that softened her. Its power can set free the hardest of sinners.

Preaching the Cross must be 'whosoever' preaching. It is for "every one". Mediate for a moment on those two words! It is for the Jew first. It is for the Greek. It is for the Barbarians (someone speaking another language). It is for the wise man. It is for the unwise man. It is for King Agrippa. It is for Onesimus the slave. It is for Felix the governor. It is for the chief man Publius. It is for "every one".

When a man stands with the Word of God and preaches the Cross, Satan trembles. The argument has gone to a new level. It is no longer our wisdom and our intellect and our persuasion, it is now God and His power doing the work. We make a grave mistake when we leave the dynamite home, for without the preaching of the Cross, we fight a battle we cannot win.

God never asked for our analysis, our approval, or our advice. Our day brings so many new ideas we may well have forgotten one old, old story of Jesus and His love. Should we return to preaching Christ and the Cross, we just might make a remarkable discovery.

We might just realize it's powerful!

Chapter Seven
Who Do They Think They Are?

"...hath not God made foolish the wisdom of this world?"
1 Corinthians 1:20

PAUL HAD 'EM. We have 'em. People who think they are smarter than God. In 1 Corinthians 1:20, they are described by three questions. "Where is the wise? where is the scribe? where is the disputer of this world?"

These three classes of scholars were the experts in their field - the best that society could produce. The wise man was the clever man, perhaps a Greek philosopher whose talks would send the masses away reveling in what they heard. The scribe was a Jewish expert of the law. Unlike most Pharisees who were unpaid 'experts', the scribes were paid for their knowledge. They were Pharisees on steroids. The disputers were the best of the Greek and Jewish world. They loved the argument and would take any side in order to engage the debate.

God said there was one thing they had in common. All three classes were "of this world." No matter how many degrees they earned, no matter how many seminars they attended, they were still of this world. They may have been the best this world could offer, but they were still limited.

It is easy to be intimidated by profound discourse and numerous degrees. A humble preacher of the cross may feel inadequate to engage in such a conversation, but God was not so easily daunted. The three questions of verse 20 have a ring of ridicule to them. There is a sense of Psalm 2:4 here: "He that sitteth in the heavens shall laugh: the Lord shall have them in derision." Similarly in Isaiah 19:12 and 33:18, God is not interested in engaging them, respecting them, or seeking their approval. God is taunting them.

So while they are laughing at God, God is laughing at them! Instead of scrambling to find a new method to meet their standards, God simply responds by calling a man to preach.

"For after that in the wisdom of God the world by wisdom knew not God, it pleased God by the foolishness of preaching to save them that believe" (1 Corinthians 1:21). He turns the tables on the wise and the scholars and the debaters. While they were mocking preaching, God said it "pleased" Him. We can hear Heaven answer their sneers and sarcasm with a hearty "take that!"

Charles Spurgeon once preached what in his judgment was one of his poorest sermons. He stammered and floundered, and when he got through he felt that it had been a complete failure. He was greatly humiliated, and when he got home he fell on his knees and said, "Lord, God, Thou canst do something with nothing. Bless that poor sermon."

All through the week he uttered that prayer. He determined that the next Sunday he would redeem himself by preaching a great sermon. He studied as never before, and, sure enough, the sermon went off beautifully. At the close the people crowded about him and showered him with praise. Spurgeon went home pleased with himself, and that night he slept like a baby. He said to himself, "I'll watch the results of those two sermons."

From the one that has seemed a failure he was able to trace forty-one conversions. From that magnificent sermon he was unable to discover that a single soul was saved. He concluded that the Spirit of God used the one and did not use the other.[7]

Many churches that were built on preaching have taken a different direction. Those methods may have been acceptable in another day, but things are different now. What a great reminder to read a passage like 1 Corinthians 1, and note yet again, that "my thoughts are not your thoughts, neither are your ways my ways, saith the LORD" (Isaiah 55:8).

Perhaps as we are hanging our degrees on the wall, as we are engaging discussion on new methods and new ministries, and as we are patting each other on the back, God is having a different reaction.

He might just be laughing.

Chapter Eight

Signs and Sagacity

"But unto them which are called, both Jews and Greeks,
Christ the power of God, and the wisdom of God."
1 Corinthians 1:24

HOW DIFFICULT is the job of the Bible preacher! When I first started in evangelism, I asked a pastor how he described his job. "Do you remember going to the circus and seeing the guy spinning the plates? He would get one going, step to the next pole and start that one, move to the next pole and start that one. Before he could spin plate number four, he had to go back to pole number one and get that one going again. He would jump to pole number four and start that plate, go back to number two, on to number five, back to three, back to one, on to six and well, you get the idea. That is what it is like being a pastor."

Another pastor joked like this: "The ministry would be a great thing if there weren't any people." Most of us have a tendency to make life difficult for our preacher. Often, it is our audacity that causes us to think our ideas are better than God's ideas. As it is now, so it was in Corinth.

When Paul was preaching the Cross, there were two large contingents that did not accept the message. But not to worry Mr. Paul, they had a better idea. Like so many modern day 'experts' (an expert is defined as someone who has all the answers so they stop listening), the Jews and Greeks of Corinth had a different idea, a better way. It went like this:

"For the Jews require a sign, and the Greeks seek after wisdom" (1 Corinthians 1:22).

"Require a sign"? Who are we humans to "require" anything from God? "Shall the thing formed say to him that formed it, Why hast thou made me thus" (Romans 9:20)? The word "require" pictures someone inferior making a demand of someone who is their superior. The religious Jews had the bluster to actually demand a sign from God!

Well then, what kind of sign would you like? Perhaps you would like a baby born of a virgin? Maybe you would like to see someone heal the sick, open the eyes of the blind, cleanse lepers, and give new ears to the deaf? Would it satisfy you if someone stood if front of a tomb and called a man dead for four days back to life? Would it work if someone personally rose from the dead?

No wonder Jesus said, "A wicked and adulterous generation seeketh after a sign" (Matthew 16:4).

Nothing has changed. Compare the crowd at a local church revival meeting, where a man will open the Bible and preach the cross, with the crowd at the faith healer's meeting. No contest. People do not want the Bible. They do not want the Cross. They do, however, love apparent miracles. Ultimately, they will accept and extol the Antichrist because his "coming is after the working of

Satan with all power and signs and lying wonders" (2 Thessalonians 2:9).

Meanwhile, the Greeks in Corinth were seeking for "wisdom". What a word! The heart of Jesus meant He came to "seek" the lost man (Luke 19:10), but the pride of the Greek man meant he came to "seek" a new nugget of wisdom. They could not admit that their human thinking was inferior, hence they could never understand the greater wisdom of God.

There is no apology. There is no meeting of the minds. "But we preach Christ crucified, unto the Jews a stumblingblock, and unto the Greeks foolishness" (1 Corinthians 1:23). Preach the Cross! We cannot change the message to please the crowd. We don't have the liberty of inventing our own alternative plan.

How perfect is the preaching of the Cross!

It is a *simple* message. Christ crucified. Two words is all it takes. If a sinner wants to go to Heaven, eternal life boils down to these two words and only these two words - Christ crucified. The complexities of religion have to be abandoned. A sinner must come just as he is.

It is a *stumbling* message. A stumblingblock is a trap. The Jews were taught to believe that anyone hung upon a cross was cursed, and as such they were to be reproached and taunted, not revered (Deuteronomy 21:23). The message of faith in one who died on a cross was too much to handle, and they would stumble right over the message into Hell.

It is a *silly* message. When the Greek heard of the Cross, they dismissed it with one word - foolish. It would be foolish to think that God would allow His son to die for others. It would be foolish to think that honor could be found in such a curse. Yet, the same Greeks who laughed at Calvary, thought their own statues were powerful gods. They convinced themselves that idols made at the hands of silversmiths could bless and protect them. The ones mocking the Cross were worshipping the Creation but not the Creator.

It is a *strong* message. "But unto them which are called, both Jews and Greeks, Christ the power of God, and the wisdom of God" (1 Corinthians 1:24). The "called" are the saved of verse 18, and the believers of verse 21. We gratefully magnify our Savior who combined the power and the wisdom of God on the Cross.

Instead of new methods and ideas, let's return to the Cross. Let's go back to the simple Gospel message. The Cross needs no apologies. The Cross needs no improvements. A desperate world has convinced itself that they need a miraculous sign which will satisfy their intellect and wisdom.

God said they need "Christ crucified".

Chapter Nine
"Things" for Jesus

"He that glorieth, let him glory in the Lord."
1 Corinthians 1:31

IT WOULD STAND to reason that the message of the Cross would require a special individual to proclaim it. Human wisdom calls for the elected elite, a person trained in a select seminary, who possesses impressive intellect and demonstrates persuasive powers. The search goes on for the finest representatives who will raise the level of discussion with their polished style and loquacious fluency. Only the best will do!

Not surprisingly, God has a different standard. A common message of the Cross will not work from the vocal chords of a religious highbrow who is more interested in impressing humans than pleasing God. Since the lost world calls preaching *"foolishness"*, and they call Calvary *"foolishness"*, the insignificant man who preaches the Cross should expect to be considered a fool as well.

In fact, if he is not a fool, he is not a man chosen of God. "For ye see your calling, brethren, how that not many wise men after the flesh, not many mighty, not many noble, are called: But God hath chosen the foolish things of the world to confound the wise; and God hath chosen the weak things of the world to confound the things which are mighty; And base things of the world, and things which are despised, hath God chosen, yea, and things which are not, to bring to nought things that are" (1 Corinthians 1:26-28).

We have a "calling". The glorious Savior has extended a supremely generous invitation to a lowly man. What an honor! What a privilege! That calling is *"your"* calling. It is a very personal invitation for a feeble human to invest his life in preaching Christ! Who could possibly say no? A man does not have to be respected for his wisdom (though he might be). A man does not have to be mighty or noble (though they are welcome to come). He just has to be willing.

We are "chosen". The word is used three times for emphasis and what an emphasis it is. He is willing to choose the "foolish", the "weak", the "base", and the "despised". What a lineup for Jesus!

God is telling the wise man that if he wants to go to Heaven, then Mr. Fool has a message for him. God is telling the mighty man that Mr. Weak is ready to explain to him that he is not strong enough to save himself. To the man of noble birth, the Lord presents Mr. Base, some boorish man from the wrong side of the tracks, who is ready to point out that a sinner coming to Christ must humble himself.

Who does God use? Things! Foolish things. Weak things. Base things. Despised things.

'Things' for Jesus! Anybody can do that!

When the eloquent man delivers an impressive homily, the people praise the man. When the legendary athlete or honored politician gives his shallow testimony, they gush over his greatness. When the talented musician puts on a show for the ages, they respond with a standing ovation.

When 'things' exalt Jesus, the glory does not go to a human, it goes to the Savior. "He that glorieth, let him glory in the Lord" (1 Corinthians 1:31). We have so much applause for people on Sunday morning, there is nothing left over for the Lord of Lords. We have so many titles and honors and degrees bestowed upon men, there are no fitting titles left to magnify Him. But nobody claps for 'things.' Nobody gives an honorary degree to a little ole' 'thing.'

A 'thing' for Jesus! Anybody can qualify for that.

I have an uncle who long ago graduated to Heaven, but not before preaching to millions of people. Pick your most popular evangelist with packed stadiums, and my uncle gave the Gospel to more people than most of them put together.

You never heard of my uncle. After all, he was just a 'thing.'

When Jesus saved him, he was so full of gratitude for Christ, he wanted the world to know the Savior. But he was so quiet, shy, and humble, there was no way he could ever stand in a pulpit and give his name, let alone preach a message.

But 'things' find a way. For years, my uncle would strap a sandwich board over his shoulders. The front side said, "Ye must be born again." The back side said, "Search the

Scriptures." He took his sign and walked back and forth through Times Square in New York City, letting the words preach to millions.

One particular gentleman saw the sign, and the words "Ye must be born again" penetrated his heart. He asked his Lutheran pastor the meaning of the verse, and was told, "Norm, you are all right. We took care of that when we baptized you as a baby."

The Lord would not let him loose. He could not escape the power of the Bible and the conviction of the Holy Spirit. It was not long before he understood John 3, bowed his knee to Christ, and was gloriously saved. Norm Ericson is now Missionary Norm Ericson. He's just another 'thing' serving Jesus.

A 'thing' for Jesus. I can do that. You can do that. If we understand it doesn't matter who does the job, so long as Christ gets the credit, we can serve Him.

We can be a 'thing' for Him!

Chapter Ten
"Give 'em the Bible!"

"That your faith should not stand in the wisdom of men,
but in the power of God."
1 Corinthians 2:5

1 CORINTHIANS 2 is the homiletics class for the ages. The Apostle Paul, a mighty voice for Christ and His Word, lays out the program for a Bible preacher. If we will preach with conviction, then we must have conviction about preaching. The choice preachers talk about preaching, pray about preaching, think about preaching, read about preaching, and are consumed by preaching. Preaching is not something we do. Preaching is what we are.

"And I, brethren, when I came to you, came not with excellency of speech or of wisdom, declaring unto you the testimony of God. For I determined not to know any thing among you, save Jesus Christ, and him crucified. And I was with you in weakness, and in fear, and in much trembling" (1 Corinthians 2:1-4).

There is the purpose of preaching. Preaching is the reason we come. Paul did not come to socialize, to hunt, to play golf, to visit museums, or to eat at nice restaurants. He came to preach. Preaching changes the program. A pastor, despite his voluminous workload, must focus like a laser beam on those moments he will stand in God's pulpit. An evangelist, a missionary, or another guest preacher has to realize his mission is to be ready and able to preach.

That means God's preacher has to be a workman in the study, laboring over the Word of God. There must be a filling of his personal life with the Bible so that the message can be filled with the Bible. There must be a serious effort of prayer both for the preaching and the hearers. It is time consuming. It will wear a man out physically. There are no shortcuts.

There is the declaration of preaching. Paul did not come to 'share what the Lord laid on his heart.' Paul did not come to 'discuss relevant material.' Paul did not come to debate the leading religious experts. He came to declare the Bible, which he believed to be the written testimony of God (a conviction that intensifies a man and his message). The word "testimony" means the Bible is both the witness of God and the proof of God. As a man of God is preaching the Bible, it is the same as if God is standing in the courtroom of the Heavens, and testifying to the truth of the message. With spiritual ears, a Bible preacher can hear the 'Amen' of Glory attesting to message he preaches.

There stands the reason we "preach the word" (2 Timothy 4:2). It is the book that will never return "void" (Isaiah 55:11). It is the validation of the preacher. A preacher is not right because he is funny. A preacher is not right because he is entertaining. A preacher is not right because he is intellectual. A preacher is not right because he draws a big crowd. A preacher is right when the Bible authenticates the message. "Thy word is truth" (John 17:17)!

There is the attitude of preaching. Paul made a determination meaning he settled something in his mind. He made the choice that he had to preach the crucified Christ, because the Corinthian people most certainly needed to hear about the crucified Christ. It is the bottom line of preaching. It really doesn't matter then what the topic is, the message needs to head to the Cross.

Charles Spurgeon said, "The sermon which does not lead to Christ, or of which Jesus Christ is not the top and the bottom, is a sort of sermon that will make the devils in hell laugh, but make the angels of God weep." Jesus is always the right place to start. He is always the right place to finish. In fact, He is really the "all, and in all" (Colossians 3:11).

There is the weakness of preaching. What an admission. Paul had some physical weakness that caused others to find fault. He may have had a voice that sounded funny (perhaps that was his "thorn in the flesh"). He may have stammered. Whatever the "weakness" may have been, it was enough to intimidate him. When he stood up to preach, he was so petrified, he would literally begin to tremble. Imagine that! Of all people, the Apostle Paul couldn't preach without having a panic attack!

Look at the preachers that God is using. Not too many have Hollywood looks. Not too many have an overabundance of grace and charm. Very few have great business opportunities pulling them in a different direction. It would be shocking to publicly know the insecurities that so many of God's men have when they stand up to preach, yet they are overcome by the immense realization that a man of God must "preach the word".

When I first entered the fields of evangelism, the respected and beloved evangelist Monroe Parker was gracious enough to join me for lunch. When I asked what words of advice he had for a young preacher, he smiled and said these words:

"Brother! Just give 'em the Bible!"

"So Doctor Paul, you have started scores of churches. You have been used of God to pen a great portion of the New Testament. You have given yourself to His work so that your physical body bears the marks of the Cross. You have been run out of town, fought with the beasts, and been imprisoned. You have seen it all, heard it all, and experienced it all. Do you have any advice for us?"

"Brother! Just give 'em the Bible!"

Chapter Eleven

Enticing Words

"And my speech and my preaching was not with enticing words
of man's wisdom, but in demonstration of the Spirit and of power:"
1 Corinthians 2:4

EVERY TIME we stand in God's pulpit, we would do well
to remind ourselves that we have been "put in trust with
the Gospel" (1 Thessalonians 2:4). God has delegated to us
the consummate message of the peerless Savior. A man
standing to preach the Gospel has a greater responsibility
than the President of the United States giving a State of the
Union address. Abraham Lincoln said, "There is nothing
so great under heaven as to be the ambassador of Christ."
The message of Christ crucified will set the course for an
individual's eternity. Heaven or Hell depends on what is
done with Christ.

As God has put us in trust with the Gospel, we must be
careful when handling that Gospel. An unprepared man
standing in the pulpit without study and prayer fails to
understand what he is doing to Christ. It is impossible to
imagine a more important, a more sober enterprise than
preaching the Word, yet the world is full of careless and
lazy preachers delivering lifeless messages. If Christ, who
was rich, became poor for me, so that I "through his

poverty might be rich" (2 Corinthians 8:9), then He deserves the best when I am standing in the pulpit.

1 Corinthians 2 teaches that a preacher has a choice to make: "And my speech and my preaching was not with enticing words of man's wisdom, but in demonstration of the Spirit and of power: That your faith should not stand in the wisdom of men, but in the power of God" (1 Corinthians 2:4-5).

I can preach with "enticing" words. Enticing words are humanly persuasive words. Those words may be delivered with humor, with smoothness, with theatrics, but the end result is a hearer being persuaded by a human minister. The preacher may be loud, he may be soft, but he is trying to convince people of his own opinion.

Note the pair of words in the verse. My "speech" and my "preaching". Preaching can be enticing based on the style of the preacher or by the content of what is preached. Someone may leave a meeting saying, "What a preacher he is!" Another may say, "What a message that was!"

People should be saying, "What a Savior we have!"

"Enticing" words are the result of human wisdom. A preacher is convinced that he has a 'great truth' that the people need to hear. No one knows where this 'great truth' came from, but he has convinced himself that because he has thought it, it must be true, and it must be from God. After all, "I wouldn't have thought of it if it wasn't right!" He stands up on Sunday to preach his 'great truth', ignoring the fact the Bible never says, "Preach a great truth." It says, "Preach the Word!"

I can preach in demonstration of the Spirit and power. Such preaching won't leave them impressed with me, but they will be in awe of the power of God. There is only one way to preach the power of God, and that is to preach the Bible. "For the word of God is quick, and powerful, and sharper than any twoedged sword" (Hebrews 4:12). It is not enough to preach about the Bible. It is not enough to refer to the Bible. It is not enough to preach what is contained in the Bible. Every time a man that has been entrusted with the Gospel stands in a pulpit that does not belong to him, to preach to a church of which Jesus is the head, he had better be certain he is accurately preaching the Bible and not human truth.

In 17th century England, 'pudding' contained the entrails of a pig, sheep, or other animal, stuffed with a mixture of minced meat, oatmeal, and seasonings. It was hardly the chocolate pudding we are used to. As such, before a family would partake, it would behoove someone to test the pudding, as it could be potentially hazardous. From those taste tests came the saying, "The proof of the pudding is in the eating."

The Bible says the proof of the preaching is in the product. Enticing preaching leads to church members standing in the wisdom of men, who are convinced "it is true because my pastor says it is true." Bible preaching leads to church members who have powerful lives of victory. They will say, "It is true because the Bible says so."

Given enough time, the preaching will produce a product. Strong preaching produces strong people. Soft preaching produces soft people. Critical preaching produces critical people. Lazy preaching produces lazy people. Cynical preaching produces cynical people. Shallow preaching produces shallow people. Emotional preaching produces emotional people. Balanced preaching produces balanced people. Simple preaching produces simple people.

Most importantly, Bible preaching will produce Bible people.

A young pastor frequently observes a spiritually strong church and wonders how it was built. He will notice that 90% of the Sunday morning crowd is back on Sunday night, and the Wednesday night crowd is about the same. He notices impressive young people serious about the will of God. There is a healthy respect for righteousness without an attitude of pharisaism. The families are strong. People know what they believe.

"What is the secret? What does that pastor know that I don't know? How did he do that?"

There is no special program, no seminar to attend. The answer is quite simple. If you want people to stand in the power of God, then you must build them on the Word of God. That takes a lot of time, a lot of patience, and a lot of Bible.

In the end, we must have this goal: "Your faith should not stand in the wisdom of men, but in the power of God."

Chapter Twelve

Preaching with the Wisdom of God

"But we speak the wisdom of God in a mystery, even the hidden wisdom, which God ordained before the world unto our glory:"
1 Corinthians 2:7

"MY BOY," said the store owner to his new employee, "wisdom and integrity are essential to the retail business. By 'integrity' I mean if you promise a customer something, you have got to keep that promise - even if it means we lose money." "And what," asked the teenager, "is wisdom?" "That," answered the boss, "is not making any stupid promises."[8]

Wise people are known by their tongue. "The tongue of the wise useth knowledge aright" (Proverbs 15:2). In a world that is so quick to get even, foolish people have a tendency to dig their hole a little deeper with hasty words, but the "words of a wise man's mouth are gracious" (Ecclesiastes 10:12).

God's preachers have a tremendous responsibility to speak wisdom. Auditoriums of people are in dire need of words from the mouthpiece of God that will affect their lives. Evil philosophies full of human logic and worldly conclusions are drawing them down a path of confusion, leaving them desperate for the wisdom of God.

That wisdom gives someone the skill to live a life that is pleasing and honoring to Him. That skill goes much further than an impressive knowledge about God; it works itself out in the way a man lives his life. 'Wisdom of God' preaching gets down to Main Street where people live. It tells a child of God how to beat the flesh, how to have the joy of the Lord, and how to make godly decisions. It will bring the Bible from the pulpit to the everyday lives of people.

In 1 Corinthians 2, Paul was not only concerned with the style of his preaching, but also with the content. He wanted to be certain the convicting factor was not his own "excellency of speech", or "enticing words" but rather the Spirit of God. He recognized the only way to accomplish such a goal was to "speak the wisdom of God in a mystery, even the hidden wisdom, which God ordained before the world unto our glory" (1 Corinthians 2:7). In a city full of intellectualism and human thinking, Paul taught the Corinthian church how to preach with God's wisdom:

Recognize that God's Wisdom will never be found in the world. The warning in the Bible says, "The wisdom of this world...(and) of the princes of this world...(will come) to nought" (1 Corinthians 2:6). The enlightenment of this world, as housed in its scholarship and universities, cannot give spiritual wisdom. The leaders of education, politics, and entertainment adhere to a worldly philosophy which has rejected the authority of God.

There cannot be a successful combination of the world's wisdom and God's wisdom. It has to be one or the other. We must understand that the wisdom of this world will come to "nought", it will surely pass away and become invalidated. History proves that. A teaching once considered cutting-edge, often becomes a distant memory most likely impugned. God's word never changes.

Too many preachers, in the name of scholarship, have tried to mix the 'wisdom' of the experts with the Bible. It cannot be done. The lost scientist will never give his stamp of approval to a message on Creation. The pagan psychologist will never agree with the notion that there are "wages of sin." The liberal minister cannot find middle ground with "thy word is truth."

When God's man studies his Bible, he must be certain he is seeking God's truth. There is a place for commentaries, dictionaries, and human authors, but they never supersede the Bible, as the greatest commentary on the Bible is the Bible. A man who spends more time studying the experts' opinions about the Bible than in the Bible itself will soon sound more like a professor than a Bible preacher.

A preacher must stand in the pulpit with a firm grasp both of his message and the hearers. When Jesus preached, the "common people heard him gladly" (Mark 12:37). The religious establishment responded like this: "The scribes and the Pharisees began to urge him vehemently, and to provoke him to speak of many things: Laying wait for him, and seeking to catch something out of his mouth, that they might accuse him" (Luke 11:53-54).

Years ago, I visited a large church whose ministry included a seminary. A visiting minister preached the Sunday morning service on the *"Critical Qualities of the*

Hypostatic Union". The message may have impressed the esteemed professors, but the common man left the building unmoved.

When we stand in a pulpit that does not belong to us, we must recognize that God has not called us to deliver an impressive speech. He has called us to preach a message that has not been mixed with or stained by the world's thinking. A message based on the world's expertise is not a message of God.

Recognize that God's Wisdom is a mystery to the unsaved man. Though a preacher of the Bible has a responsibility to preach so his listeners can get the message, the paradox still remains. No matter how simple the message or how clearly it is delivered, it will still fall on the ears of people that are spiritually deaf. We are speaking "the wisdom of God in a mystery." To the lost man it is a "hidden wisdom" (1 Corinthians 2:7).

It can be frustrating to watch an unsaved man sit in a church pew for years and never respond to the Bible. He will reject invitation after invitation, disheartening the preacher. It seems so simple to us. "Ye must be born again." "Believe on the Lord Jesus Christ." The words are so transparent, a little child can get them, but to an unsaved man, they may as well be Egyptian hieroglyphics. It is a great "mystery". Only the Spirit of God can break down those barriers.

It is important to preach from the perspective of the unsaved man. Good preachers will anticipate the reaction of the sinner and answer them accordingly. They will say: "Perhaps some of you are thinking ..."; "Some may say ...";

Like a good lawyer predicting a potential response, they will head off the argument at the pass.

We must be careful about terms that are familiar to us but not to the sinner. We have our own vocabulary, but words that fill our songs and sermons are unusual and strange to the unsaved man. "Saved" and "born again" are a daily part of our conversations, and since they are from the Bible, they must be preached, but they must be patiently explained to hearers that do not understand.

Recognize that God's Wisdom is inseparable from Calvary. Christ was slain by the wisdom of God, a sacrifice that was "ordained before the world unto our glory." Therefore, we can only preach the Wisdom of God appropriately through the lens of the Cross.

Once again, there is a mighty paradox. The Cross itself divides the wisdom of God from the wisdom of the world. They meet here to do battle. The wisdom of the world told them to crucify "the Lord of glory" (1 Corinthians 2:8). The wisdom of God points to the Cross as the "power" to save the lost man and sustain the saved man.

As we prepare to preach, we must always look at a text in its relationship to the Cross. The Old Testament stories and prophecies are validated at the Cross. The New Testament instructions for the local church are empowered by the Cross. A message for a lost man must go to the Cross, and a message to motivate the saint must find a way to bring him back to 'Calvary love.' The Christian family is founded on the Cross. The Christian teenager has a life to live because of Calvary. The discouraged man and the burdened woman are strengthened at the Cross. The topic, the exposition, and the message itself are tied together by the sacrifice of Christ.

Recognize that God's Wisdom is given to those who love Him. "But as it is written, Eye hath not seen, nor ear heard, neither have entered into the heart of man, the things which God hath prepared for them that love him." Usually, this verse is used to describe the glories of Heaven that await the saved, but that application pulls the verse out of context. The "things" prepared for the people of God are not for the sweet by and by, they are for the bitter now and now. The "things" are His masterful wisdom He desires to give those who love Him.

The normal methods used by the world for obtaining wisdom are bypassed. It will not be taught by a teacher in a classroom. It will not be found in a book at the store. God's wisdom will not "enter into" (it will not ascend with some mighty, heavenly thoughts) a man's heart. When we love Him we want to know Him. When we want to know Him, He will reveal Himself to us through His Word.

We cannot possibly preach the wisdom of God with cold hearts. If we have left our "first love" (Revelation 2:4), our personal lives will be powerless, our preaching will be feeble, and our product will be impotent. Before we can bring the saint and the sinner to the foot of the Cross, we must spend time there ourselves.

Recognize that God's Wisdom is already prepared. We do not have the capacity to dispense wisdom that changes hearts. Only God can do that. Even better, God has already done that!

The Bible is God's Wisdom. Simply yet powerfully, 1 Corinthians 2:8-9 detail its authority and wonder. Human eyes have never witnessed an experience like the Bible. Human ears have never heard a lecture like the message of the Bible. Human hearts have never received truth like the perfection of the Bible.

The Bible is prepared for us. Note the past tense of the verb. The phrase cannot be speaking of Heaven, because He is presently preparing a place for us. The completed, perfect, authoritative Word of God is a finished product. And He did it all for us. Through the millennia of time, despite multitudes of attacks and enemies, He carefully made understandable the infinite wisdom of God. All we need to know is in that Book!

The Bible is God's revelation given by the Spirit of God. He has chosen to peel back the curtains of mystery that are hidden to us. Godly people don't look to dreams and visions for God's revelations; they go to the Bible. Opinions constantly change but the Bible is permanent.

It is impossible to overestimate the importance of Bible preaching. If a listener leaves the auditorium with the words of a man ringing in their ears, the end result is human produced. When someone walks away with the Bible in their hearts, they have been infused with the wisdom of God. There is no substitute for studying the Bible and declaring the Bible.

Recognize that God's Wisdom flows from God's Spirit. The spiritual truth of the Bible cannot be comprehended apart from the Spirit of God working in our hearts. The "deep things" of God are impossible to grasp until we have submitted ourselves to the Spirit of God, taking the Word of God and applying it to our lives.

We are stunned when unsaved people twist the Bible in ridiculous ways and wonder how anyone can possibly come to the conclusions they do. We channel surf and listen for a few moments to the false minister, Joel Osteen. We shake our heads amazed that anyone could pay heed to such spiritual gibberish, but they do - to the tune of 10 million viewers a week. How is it possible that anyone would swallow the line of Benny Hinn after his phony act has been debunked? His wife divorces him, while he is speaking his son is arrested for assaulting one of the listeners; his phony healing 'ministry' is repeatedly exposed, yet his books sell by the millions.

Why do people refuse the eternal words preserved and protected by God and replace them with lying pronouncements from charlatans? The answer is simple: "But the natural man receiveth not the things of the Spirit of God: for they are foolishness unto him: neither can he know them, because they are spiritually discerned" (1 Corinthians 2:14). Because they do not have the Spirit of God, they do not have the "mind of Christ," so they rely on human thinking which deceives them every time.

A man of God preaching the Word of God must be absolutely dependent on the Spirit of God. It is important to slow down when studying the Bible and meditate on single verses and phrases. Compare "spiritual things with spiritual." Use the Bible to understand the Bible, and ask the Spirit of God to illuminate difficult passages of the Bible.

Ask His help in understanding what people need. Individuals fill an auditorium carrying issues that we know nothing of, but the Spirit of God knows. We don't even know what to pray for, but the Holy Spirit always gets it right (Romans 8:26). As we study the Bible and prepare a message, the constant prayer must be, "What do I need? What do the people need?" Our helplessness is conquered by the Spirit of the Living God.

The evangelist of yesteryear, D.L. Moody, put it like this:

My friends, we have too many orators in the pulpit. I am tired and sick of your "silver-tongued orators." I used to mourn because I couldn't be an orator. I thought, Oh, if I could only have the gift of speech like some men! I have heard men with a smooth flow of language take the audience captive; but they came and they went. Their voice was like the air—there wasn't any power back of it; they trusted in their eloquence and their fine speeches. That is what Paul was thinking of when he wrote to the Corinthians: "My speech and my preaching was not with enticing words of man's wisdom, but in demonstration of the Spirit and of power: that your faith should not stand in the wisdom of men, but in the power of God."[9]

At the end of the day, a pastor may not have the biggest church, the greatest crowd, the fame and honors bestowed by men, but if he has been true to the Bible, obedient to the Spirit of God, he will produce a people that are standing in the power of God.

A "well done, *thou* good and faithful servant" will make it all worthwhile.

Chapter Thirteen
Number 1

"...as unto carnal, even as unto babes..."
1 Corinthians 3:1

ONE WORD SUMS it up. All the envying and battles and divisions of chapter one were described by that simple word. I suspect the members of the Paul camp and the Apollos camp and the Cephas camp and the super-spiritual Christ camp saw themselves differently, but God described them like this:

"Carnal".

We normally define the word in a sensual manner, but that is a mistake. The word pictures a person dominated by self-esteem, doing whatever is necessary to be successful. Carnal people are not necessarily immoral people; they are people that follow their own impulses and drives. They are convinced their ideas are not only the best ideas, they are the only ideas.

Carnal people have to be 'number 1.'

By definition, there can only be one 'number 1.' If a pastor is 'number 1' then Jesus is not. If a deacon is 'number 1,' then Jesus is not. If a singer is 'number 1,' then Jesus is not. There is room for only one at the top.

A preacher needs to be constantly exalting Christ, placing Him on the pedestal of the local church by consistently preaching on His preeminence and glory. Conversely, he needs to be on guard against the divisions and enemies that are so quick to promote their agendas and doctrine. The carnal Christian must be exposed!

"And I, brethren, could not speak unto you as unto spiritual, but as unto carnal, even as unto babes in Christ. I have fed you with milk, and not with meat: for hitherto ye were not able to bear it, neither yet now are ye able. For ye are yet carnal: for whereas there is among you envying, and strife, and divisions, are ye not carnal, and walk as men? For while one saith, I am of Paul; and another, I am of Apollos; are ye not carnal?" (1 Corinthians 3:1-4)

The Bible describes the condition of the carnal man as a baby. What a startling message that must have been to the 'spiritual giants' of Corinth. Convinced of their superiority, they were constantly lording over the more humble members of the church, yet they were not all they were cracked up to be.

They were such infants, someone like Paul had to bottle feed them. They were too tiny to comprehend any new spiritual truth, settling for a diet of skim milk when they could have been feasting on prime rib. They had a spiritual version of the 'Peur Aeturnus Complex', a description given to a man who refuses to grow up. Stunted in their Christian lives, they were living in the past and going nowhere. There is nothing wrong with being a spiritual baby, but there is everything wrong with staying a spiritual baby. Such infants produce callow churches.

Like all babies, there was one 'ministry' in which they excelled. They knew how to make big messes! Their church was shredded by incessant envy which produced strife and division. Instead of fighting the devil, they were fighting each other, creating a split church, and forcing Paul to expose and isolate them. In so doing, he provided powerful lessons for today's preacher:

Preach on the 'nothingness' of humans. Who do we think we are? The factions of Corinth were so impressed with their chosen leaders, but Paul knew his place! He saw himself as the plowboy and Apollos as the water boy!

"Who then is Paul, and who is Apollos, but ministers by whom ye believed, even as the Lord gave to every man? I have planted, Apollos watered; but God gave the increase. So then neither is he that planteth any thing, neither he that watereth; but God that giveth the increase." (1 Corinthians 3:5-7)

When Paul was tempted to think of himself "more highly than he ought to think" (Romans 12:3), all he needed to do was look at his ID. He would be reminded that when God saved him, He changed his identity, giving him a new name. Saul (meaning ask for; demanded) was changed to Paul (meaning little). He was a big man in the religious scheme before he was saved, but Jesus turned him into a fool. Now he was a little man, happy in the service of his eminent King.

Preach on the 'bigness' of God. While we are nothing, He is everything. He gives the "increase." We are so prone to think the work is ours, and that results depend on our efforts, but all the good work is done by God. We may plant the seed or water the ground, but the fruit is His. We are His sheep. It is His pasture.

God's preachers make much of God. Our music needs to magnify Him. Our words need to exalt Him. Our messages need to lift Him up. Our feeble tongues cannot possibly do Him justice, yet with our best efforts He must be praised.

Preach on the foundation of Christ. "For other foundation can no man lay than that is laid, which is Jesus Christ" (1 Corinthians 3:11). A church built on Paul would be a disaster. A church built on Peter would quickly move to apostasy. A church built on Christ will stand against the "gates of hell" (Matthew 16:18). The music program, the youth program, the seniors program, the bus ministry, the Sunday School, the Christian School, and every other ministry must be built on Christ. He is the one and only foundation.

When Hudson Taylor prepared young missionaries for service in his mission, he insisted, "Remember that when you come out here you are *nothing*. It is only what God can and will do through you that will be worth anything." One young missionary replied, "It is hard for me to believe that I am just nothing." Taylor said to him, "Take it by faith because it is true - you are nothing."[10]

There is room for one Savior. There is room for one God. The carnal Christian wants to be number one, but there is no place for such a person in the Savior's local church.

Chapter Fourteen
Critics

"MIne answer to them that do examine me..."
1 Corinthians 9:3

THE SUPER SPIRITUAL in Corinth failed to see rampant immorality infecting the church, yet they were quick to criticize others. They were infatuated with their own liberty yet unconcerned about their influence on the weaker brother. Such people are never wrong, do not receive correction, and are ready to pounce on anyone who will dare suggest they are a problem. Blinded to their own condition, they are ready to impart their wisdom to the masses and expose the sins of others. They are experts in criticism.

Years ago, I was preaching a revival meeting on the east coast, and I was introduced to a man with a rather unusual 'ministry.' I have been honored to meet thousands of people that tirelessly work for Christ in their church, volunteering countless hours. I have witnessed numerous ministries, even some that were a little unique, but this gentleman had a 'ministry' I had never heard of.

He believed that God had called him to be a critic of preachers.

I am quite certain that every church has a cadre of folks like him, but there are not many who readily admit it. He did. He genuinely thought that God had saved him for the purpose of criticizing preachers. After all, NFL teams have their talk radio critics. Hollywood has its movie critics. Why shouldn't Baptist preachers have their very own critics?

This is nothing new. In 1 Corinthians 9, Paul had his critics. Now it might seem that a man who was saved from the strongholds of Judaism, been entrusted with the precious words of the Bible in penning a great portion of the New Testament, had been allowed of God to establish scores of churches, and had given his body to be burned, might be spared the poison of the critic. Not so! The spiritual elite in Corinth knew what they were called to do! They had responded to the call of God! They knew their ministry.

They were called to "examine" him (1 Corinthians 9:3).

It was their responsibility to put him under the microscope and find some error. It was their job to build a case against him, to warn the brothers of the compromises of the Apostle Paul. Amazingly, they did it without a webpage or a blog.

Paul was ready for them, and in so doing, he gave a preacher his marching orders in dealing with criticism.

Build a history. In 14 verses he asks 18 rhetorical questions, each one exposing the charges of the critics as ridiculous and petty. He started like this: "Am I not an apostle? am I not free? have I not seen Jesus Christ our Lord? are not ye my work in the Lord" (1 Corinthians 9:1)?

He is saying, "As you well know, I am an apostle. As you well know, I am free. As you well know, I have seen Christ. As you well know, you are my work in the Lord."

As an apostle, Paul had power and influence beyond any in Corinth, yet he did not flaunt that position, because he was far more concerned about the weaker brother. As a free man, Paul had the privilege to exercise more liberty than someone in Corinth, but he used his freedom to limit himself. As a successful man, Paul had fruit. The church in Corinth was visible proof of the Hand of God upon him, the seal (a legally valid attestation) of his apostleship, a seal stamped by God Himself.

It takes time to build a history, but when a critic attacks a man of God, he simply needs to point to the pew. "Mr. Critic, I have invested my life in people. God has placed his stamp of approval upon the work. Take a look!" I enjoy sitting on the platform and listening to a pastor pointing out trophies of grace in the auditorium. Those stories are his history.

By the way Mr. Critic, where are your stories?

Give an answer. Some preachers shrug their shoulders when they are under attack and assume that God will defend them, yet that is not the example of Paul. "Mine answer to them that do examine me is this". His answer is commonly called an apologetic. He defended himself.

His answer was personal. He called it "mine" answer. Paul took an attack on his apostleship as serious business, not because his pride was at stake, but the work of God was assaulted. The same man who patiently suffered personally for Christ refused to allow the local church to be injured.

Defend your church. We would have no respect for a father who refused to defend his children. We have no respect for the spineless generation that has tossed our blood-bought American freedoms down the sewer of liberalism. When a New Testament Local Church, bought with the precious blood of Christ is assaulted by demonic forces, it is not time to be a pacifist. Paul was ready. "Mine answer...is this."

Never surrender your soul liberty. In 1 Corinthians 9:4-6, there are three occasions where Paul refers to the "power" he has been blessed with. That "power" is the authority God had invested in him to properly perform the work of God. The super spiritual in Corinth were ultimately attacking the authority he had from God, and had they been successful, they would have inflicted great damage.

Paul had the soul liberty to expect the church to meet the financial needs so that he could "eat and...drink". He had the liberty to "lead" his family according to the direction of God, not the demands of the brethren. He had the power to establish a set of financial convictions. Paul and Barnabas, (evidently they had patched things up), had decided to stop working and give themselves to the ministry, expecting God to meet their needs through the churches. As Barnabas was a wealthy landowner, it is likely that Christians as touchy as the Corinthians thought it rather presumptuous for a man of considerable means to take advantage of their hospitality. If he was going to be a preacher of the gospel, they might have said, the least he could do was pay his own way.

Don't let a backslidden church member rob your joy and make you miserable. You have the precious gift of liberty to build a Christ honoring ministry dedicated to Him. Never allow the critic to demand you follow his carnal and childish whims, meeting their human standard. A critic is only happy when he can cause someone else to be as miserable as he.

Go to the Bible. Paul uses the Word in a fascinating way. He asks, "Doth God take care for oxen?" (1 Corinthians 9:9) God cares for the beasts of the field and expects humans to care for them as well. More importantly, if we tend to animals, should churches not care for those who minister to them?

The critics claimed that Paul and Barnabas were able to work and care for themselves, but the Bible differed with their human reasoning. The best way to silence the long tongue of the critic is to open the book and give them the Bible.

Build a testimony above reproach. It is true that Paul had a right to their financial help, but he refused it. "Nevertheless we have not used this power; but suffer all things, lest we should hinder the gospel of Christ" (1 Corinthians 9:12). " But I have used none of these things" (1 Corinthians 9:15).

For their sakes, it was important they gave the money. For the Gospel's sake, it was important that Paul refuse to use it for himself. We can hear him say, "I have refused your gifts for the Gospel. I do not want a lost man to use me as an excuse to reject Christ!"

The critics, then and now, usually focus their attack on financial issues, so it is imperative we do not give them any ammunition. A preacher should be nowhere near the offering. There has to be accountability and then more accountability. Satan's skeptics love to look under the carpet for dirty money, so be certain there is nothing there when they come looking.

Two taxidermists stopped before a window in which an owl was on display. They immediately began to criticize the way it was mounted. Its eyes were not natural; its wings were not in proportion with its head; its feathers were not neatly arranged; its feet could be improved. When they had finished with their criticism, the old owl turned his head and winked at them.[11]

Those two can be found many a Sunday in church pews ready to inflict their poison. Don't let them get the victory. Don't let them drag the church down. Don't let them be tools of Satan.

Wink at them.

Chapter Fifteen

Preach or Die

"For though I preach the gospel, I have nothing to glory of: for necessity is laid upon me; yea, woe is unto me, if I preach not the gospel!"
1 Corinthians 9:16

"IT WERE BETTER for me to die" (1 Corinthians 9:15). "Woe is unto me" (1 Corinthians 9:16).

When God saved Paul on the Damascus Road, he abandoned his own desires for the will of God. "Lord, what wilt thou have me to do" (Acts 9:6)? For some 33 years, the Lord told him what to do, and no human has had a greater impact on the New Testament local church. He lived for serving Christ. It was a passion that consumed him.

There was a fear that constantly gnawed at him, a dread that ultimately became a great motivation. He worried he would violate the very message he preached by a stained life, and in so doing, someone would "make (his) glorying void." His "glorying" was preaching the Cross: "But God forbid that I should glory, save in the cross of our Lord Jesus Christ, by whom the world is crucified unto me, and I unto the world" (Galatians 6:14). Should the day come that he would bring disgrace and shame to the crucified Lord, Paul determined it would be better for him to die.

The name of Christ and the Cross of Calvary meant more to him than his own life.

"Better...to die."

When it came to preaching, Paul did not have a choice. Of his own ready will and ready mind (Romans 1:15), Paul surrendered all he had to Christ. When God placed him in the ministry there was no turning back, and should he ever consider quitting, there was a phrase hanging over his head.

"Woe is unto me." The word "woe" is a powerful word in the Bible. When God cries out to wicked nations and people saying "Woe unto you," He is telling them they are as good as dead. When Isaiah and Micah and Paul say, "Woe is me," they are saying, "I am as good as dead." Truly, for Paul there were two choices:

Preach or die.

There was a "necessity" laid upon Paul. A necessity is a compelling force, a word often used in the Bible to describe torture and distress. It was a pressure from above, a conviction that God laid upon him, and there was no way out. There would be no retiring, no retreating. At the end of the day there would be a guillotine.

Preach or die.

Charles Spurgeon put it like this:

I always say to young fellows who consult me about the ministry, "Don't be a minister if you can help it," because if the man can help it, God never called him. But if he cannot help it, and he must preach or die, then he is the man. [12]

Preach or die.

In the sixteenth century, there lived a minister in England by the name of Hugh Latimer. He was known as a great preacher in his day and as a result had many opportunities to speak. On one occasion, he was to preach before the King Henry VIII. As he thought about his great responsibility in standing before the king, he realized that the message that God had given him was not a message the king would want to hear.

As he began his sermon he cried, "Hugh Latimer, dost thou know before whom thou are this day to speak? To the high and mighty monarch, the king's most excellent majesty, who can take away thy life, if thou offendest. Therefore, take heed that thou speakest not a word that may displease."

Then he continued, "But then consider well, Hugh, dost thou not know from whence thou comest - upon Whose message thou are sent? Even by the great and mighty God, Who is all-present and Who beholdeth all thy ways and Who is able to cast thy soul into hell! Therefore, take care that thou deliverest thy message faithfully!" [13]

Latimer faced the choice: would he preach what man wanted to hear or would he preach what Christ would have him preach. Latimer did take his stand for truth and preached boldly. Eventually, he was martyred by Queen Mary I. [14]

Preach or die.

Chapter Sixteen

Payday

"For if I do this thing willingly, I have a reward…"
1 Corinthians 9:17

MONEY AND PREACHERS are a most intriguing combination. Everyone has a story of the good old days, when God met the financial need in miraculous ways, reminding a young pastor and his wife that as He feeds the sparrows, he remembers His own. Wonderful lessons of faith are learned for the man planting a church, for the missionary on deputation, for the evangelist hoping there is enough gas in the tank to get to the next meeting.

When I first entered into evangelism, one of the greatest impressions on me was the generosity of pastors. They would give the proverbial shirt off their backs to help meet needs of people others would ignore. Their tender hearts and generous spirit affected me profoundly.

But money has its risks. As time goes by, it is easy to forget the lessons of faith from the early days. A veteran evangelist discovers it is easy to pull on heartstrings of people during a meeting and pump a love offering. A seasoned missionary, realizing the generous spirit of many saints, takes advantage of them with letters and emails, shamelessly begging for money. A pastor finds a wealthy member in his office graciously 'suggesting' that a subtle change in his preaching will only help the church finances.

Before long, if we are not careful, money is in charge.

Every man of God comes to this crossroad, a moment when he has to decide if he is preaching for money or preaching for Christ. It may be subtle, it may seem insignificant, but the choice will set a path that will last for the remainder of his life. He will either be a servant to Jesus or Ben Franklin.

When Paul came to the crossroad, it sounded like this:

"For if I do this thing willingly, I have a reward: but if against my will, a dispensation of the gospel is committed unto me. What is my reward then? Verily that, when I preach the gospel, I may make the gospel of Christ without charge, that I abuse not my power in the gospel" (1 Corinthians 9:17-18).

The choice will come down to the will of the preacher. Standing at the point of decision, he will decide to go with his own personal will, or, he will make a choice against his will.

An evangelist following his own will slowly adopts financial policies with no accountability. Soon, he sets up a board where he is the chairman and his wife is number two. A missionary justifies the exaggerated stories that tug on the heart strings of people. Money pours into a project with no oversight. A pastor rationalizes his weakened message, convincing himself that a small change here and there will not make a great difference. "No one knows."

Sadly, our will always wills for more money. Money is an insatiable thing - there is never enough. When we follow our will, we get our "reward," yet tomorrow always seems to bring a bigger need for more money. When we make a decision based on our will, we have set a course on a highway where it becomes awfully hard to find an exit. We don't even see it happen, but pretty soon, we are no better than Balaam.

Paul saw another option. He could follow his own will and get a temporary "reward," or he could reject his own will and follow God. When he learned to make that choice, he discovered that God gave him a "dispensation." The word means to be a manager of a house. As Paul invested his life in being rich towards God, he began to understand the joy and privilege of working for Him. He realized the local church was God's house, the people were God's people, and the business was God's business. Paul saw himself as a simple caretaker.

Paul's viewpoint changes everything. An evangelist who looks across the auditorium at a church of people that belong to God cannot allow himself to preach for cash. A missionary sending a letter back to a local church where Jesus is the head will be very, very careful in asking for money to buy a new car. A pastor looking at a flock of people with Jesus as the Chief Shepherd will choose to please Him - not the backslidden, wealthy member.

Paul's priority was to "make the gospel of Christ without charge, that I abuse not my power in the gospel." He understood the potential of misusing his authority to get a reward. An evangelist, a missionary, and a pastor can easily fall into the same trap, and in so doing, they begin to charge people to hear the Gospel.

Imagine that! The wonderful salvation of God He freely gave to save us from Hell now has a price tag! The 'rockstar' preacher comes to town and sells tickets to suckers who not only fill a coliseum, they fill his pockets. They have to pay to hear him speak. A pastor brings in a big name singing group for a concert, and people have to buy tickets to come to church.

I would hate to be a preacher standing at the Judgment Seat of Christ who has to explain that!

"Well, if we didn't sell tickets, we couldn't afford to have the group come in and sing." Maybe you don't need that group to come in and sing.

So Mister Apostle Paul, what is your financial policy? I "make the gospel of Christ without charge." Then what is your payday? "That I might gain the more. If one more sinner is saved, then I will get a check that will never bounce!" He was willing to preach for free to see someone saved.

P.T. Barnum, head of the great Barnum & Bailey Circus, once invited Charles Spurgeon to speak in the large tent at his traveling circus. He made every concession to make the offer attractive, promising to provide musical talent, equipment, and manpower. Spurgeon could speak on any subject for as long as he wished, with one stipulation. Barnum Circus Association would take the gate receipts and pay him one thousand dollars per lecture, an extremely generous offer in its day. Many would doubtless have said, "What a wonderful opportunity to reach people with the Gospel!"

Pastor Spurgeon sent this reply to Mr. Barnum:

Dear Mr. Barnum:
Thank you for your kind invitation to lecture in your circus tents in America. You will find my answer in Acts 13:10.
Very sincerely yours,
Charles H. Spurgeon

If Mr. Barnum looked up Acts 13:10, he found these words: "O full of all subtility and all mischief, thou child of the devil, thou enemy of all righteousness, wilt thou not cease to pervert the right ways of the Lord?"[15]

Men like Paul and Spurgeon simply decided to postpone payday until they saw Christ. One of the most important choices we will make goes like this:

When do we want to get paid?

Chapter Seventeen
Whatever It Takes

"And this I do for the gospel's sake..."
1 Corinthians 9:23

WHEN PAUL DETERMINED that he was not preaching for money, he became a free man. The preacher who has no cash considerations going into his message can preach a lot of things others cannot and will not preach. No one owns him. He owes nobody. He can say, "I (am) free from all men" (1 Corinthians 9:19).

So Mr. Paul, now that you have this great freedom, what are you going to do with it? The answer is amazing: "For though I be free from all men, yet have I made myself servant unto all, that I might gain the more."

Imagine a slave working an entire life to gain his freedom turning around and relinquishing that freedom. Imagine a nation going to war for its independence, winning the war, then resubmitting itself to the former king. Paul had his freedom, his "liberty," yet he threw it all away, enslaving himself to others by enslaving himself to Christ. He did not want to be served; he wanted to serve.

No one in the cosmopolitan city of Corinth was exempt from his compassion. He loved the Jews, settling the

Galatian's argument that he would go to the Gentiles while James, Peter, and John would handle the Jews. He loved those who were "under the law," the Jews who followed harsh, human regulations. He loved the Gentiles who were "without the law," doing everything he could without compromising his testimony for Christ.

He loved the "weak," the humble poor of Corinth. He was willing to dress in their lowly clothes, eat their simple meals, and ignore their living conditions for the "gospel's sake." Whatever the church of Corinth was doing to reach their city, Paul wanted to be a "partaker" of the efforts. He did not expect sinners to come to him, he went to them. He was the original 'bring them in' man.

Irrespective of the social class, Paul had one goal for every citizen of Corinth. He wanted to "gain" them. It is somewhat amusing when the phrase 'soul-winning' is criticized. The modern day specialists that run to Madison Avenue for the latest techniques in church growth are highly offended by any type of confrontational efforts. "After all," they say, "the phrase soul winning is not even found in the New Testament!"

Well, the phrase soul-gaining is certainly a New Testament phrase. It is found five times in four verses, and is defined by one Greek expert as meaning "to gain, acquire as gain, to win."[16]

Paul was the consummate soul-gainer. More than claiming to love people, Paul demonstrated his compassion by paying a tremendous price for his people. That price is described in 2 Corinthians 11:24: "Of the Jews five times received I forty stripes save one."

Those beatings came with a trial, with Paul standing in a Jewish courtroom facing the charges of blasphemy. His faith in the risen Christ and his conviction that the Gospel was to the Jew first and then to the Gentiles (Romans 1:16) made the trial an open and shut case. It would not take long for the Jewish court to convict Paul, and the cry of "Guilty!" to fill the room. The Mishnah (the Jewish oral law) listed 36 sins that warranted excommunication from the Jewish community. One of those sins was blasphemy, a crime which carried the penalty that the guilty party could have no more contact with any Jew.

But there was a caveat, the 'fine print' of the Jewish law. An expelled man conceivably had the option of submitting to thirty-nine brutal lashes, a horrible flogging. It was described as such:

Floggings were administered with a whip made of calfskin on the bare upper body of the offender - one third of the lashes being given on the breast and the other two thirds on the back. The offender stood in a bowed position with the one administering the beating on a stone above him and the blows were accompanied by the recital of admonitory and consolatory verses from Scripture.[17]

Should a condemned man agree to such a beating, the law then required the Jewish community to accept him again as 'thy brother.' By surrendering to will of the court, and accepting their whipping, Paul could remain in contact with his brethren. He could witness to one more. He could lead a sinner to the Cross. All it would take was a beating that would permanently scar him, and he could go soul-gaining again.

"Paul, you have been found guilty. The law presents you with two choices. You may accept banishment, and you will have no more contact with Jews. They will be required to shun and ignore you. Or, should you prefer, you may accept a flogging of 39 stripes. Which do you choose?"

Paul chose the beating.

Five times.

Chapter Eighteen

Winners

*"I therefore so run, not as uncertainly;
so fight I, not as one that beateth the air"*
1 Corinthians 9:26

THE PARALLELS BETWEEN the preacher and the athlete abound in the Bible. Perhaps that is the reason many preachers find themselves at home on the golf course, on the tennis court, or watching a ball game. Lessons learned from the sports world have a Biblical connection with the work of the ministry.

Paul had a great love of sports, regularly using examples of runners and boxers. He loved them for another reason - they brought sinners right to him. The Corinthians, as sports-crazed as our modern society, hosted biannual contests called the Isthmus Games. Second only to the Olympics in Athens, the Isthmus games brought participants and spectators from around the world. Paul 'just happened' to be in Corinth in the Spring of AD 51 when the games were played.

In the first century, there were no permanent facilities for the massive crowds that descended upon Corinth, so for the thousands of people that flocked to Corinth, their 'home' for the week would have to be a tent. Tentmakers like Paul, Aquila, and Priscilla were in the absolute perfect location to spread the Gospel around the world.

"Know ye not that they which run in a race run all, but one receiveth the prize? So run, that ye may obtain. And every man that striveth for the mastery is temperate in all things. Now they do it to obtain a corruptible crown; but we an incorruptible. I therefore so run, not as uncertainly; so fight I, not as one that beateth the air: But I keep under my body, and bring it into subjection: lest that by any means, when I have preached to others, I myself should be a castaway" (1 Corinthians 9:24-27).

As upsetting as it may be to the modern day liberal who wants everyone to walk away a 'winner,' the Bible says that not everyone wins. Many enter the race but "one" gets the prize, which in Paul's day was a wreath or garland bestowed to the victor. No one sets out to win the Bronze medal, and in the Christian race, first runner-up is simply first loser.

The competition in our race is a little unusual. Some preachers seem to be in competition with other preachers, yet comparing ourselves among ourselves is "not wise" (2 Corinthians 10:12). This marathon race is against our own "body," our flesh. We are literally running against ourselves, the part of us that loves this world and its pleasures. Many a preacher has made their way to the starting blocks, jumped out to a good start, but failed to keep running.

The Isthmus Games had some lessons for a preacher who wants to be a winner for Christ:

A winner for Christ is a striver. A striver is someone contending in a game who believes that winning is of most importance. He is the athlete who wills himself to win, "I must win this race!" God's preacher enters the race and must beat his flesh to the finish line.

A winner for Christ is temperate. A temperate person keeps ones' impulses, emotions, and desires under control. Athletes and their trainers participating in the early Olympic games swore an oath upon slices of boar's flesh "that in nothing will they sin against the Olympic games." The athletes took this further oath, swearing that for ten successive months they have strictly followed the regulations for training. Athletes who want to win cannot conform to the world and eat the same things as those who are not preparing for the rigors of competition.[18]

If it were easy, every one would do it. Each year approximately 250,000 high school seniors participate in inter-scholastic basketball. Of these seniors, approximately 12,000 will receive college scholarships. Of those 12,000 some 200 players will be drafted by the NBA, with but 50 actually being offered a contract. Of these fifty, only five will eventually earn a starting position. Of these five, only two will stay in the NBA for more then five years.[19]

Remember how many freshman joined you at Bible College? Where are they now?

A winner for Christ is certain. He does not run "uncertainly". He has a discipline, a direction, and a design for the race. He does not run outside the lines. He does not make his own rules. He is running towards the goal (Philippians 3:14).

A winner for Christ is a fighter. The fighter does not swing wildly into the air, wasting his energy. Instead, he keeps under his body, a phrase meaning "to give oneself a black eye." Paul knew he was in the boxing ring in the midst of a great battle. There would be wounds and bruises, but that wouldn't stop him from preaching to others.

A winner for Christ is motivated. The world plays its games for corruptible crowns. As the victor's wreath was woven of oak, ivy, myrtle, olive leaves or flowers, it would soon decay. The gold medal, the Stanley Cup, the World Series trophy, and the Super Bowl trophy collect dust in a cabinet. But the crown for the victorious Christian is one that "fadeth not away" (1 Peter 5:4). God's men live for eternity.

So Paul kept pressing on. He feared becoming a "castaway" (a rejected man; a man proven to be unworthy). He dreaded the possibility that all of his preaching would be swallowed up in the pit of hypocrisy should he fall to the sin he preached against. No matter what it would take, Paul had to get to the finish line and hear, "Well done, *thou* good and faithful servant" (Matthew 25:21).

During the 1968 Mexico City Olympics, a Tanzanian marathon runner named John Stephen Akhwari had high hopes of winning the Gold. At the 19 km mark of the 42 km race, there was jockeying for position between some runners, and he was hit. He fell, badly dislocating his knee and slamming his shoulder against the pavement.

He continued running, finishing last among the 57 competitors who completed the race (75 had started). The winner of the marathon, Mamo Wolde of Ethiopia, finished in 2:20:26. When Akhwari crossed the line at the 3:25:27 mark, only a few thousand people were left in the stadium, and the sun had set. A television crew was sent out from the medal ceremony when word was received that there was one more runner about to finish.

As he finally crossed the finish line a cheer came from the small crowd. When interviewed later, and asked why he continued running, he said, "My country did not send me 5,000 miles to start the race; they sent me 5,000 miles to finish the race."[20]

My Savior did not leave Heaven's glory and go to a rugged cross for us to start the race. He did so that we might finish the race.

Chapter Nineteen

A More Excellent Way

"And now abideth faith, hope, charity, these three;
but the greatest of these is charity."
1 Corinthians 13:13

CONQUERING A CRITICAL SPIRIT and a false sense of spirituality in the local church is a difficult task. It would take something powerful in Corinth for a wealthy man to dine with a poor man, or for a landowner to be on equal footing with his most humble servant. It would demand great humility for a church member to downplay a pet peeve for the good of the assembly. It would require a more excellent way.

Paul is ready to lead the way. For 12 chapters, he has been hammering the divisiveness and carnality in the church of Corinth. He uses the word "you" or "ye" 174 times, pointing the finger of conviction, fearlessly exposing their sin. Truly, "...there is utterly a fault among you" (1 Corinthians 6:7).

Someone once said, "When you are preaching and pointing a finger at someone, remember, there are three fingers point back at yourself." 1 Corinthians 13 details the three fingers pointing back. From "you" and "ye", Paul changes the target to himself:

"Though I speak with the tongues of men and of angels, and have not charity, I am become *as* sounding brass, or a tinkling cymbal. And though I have *the gift of* prophecy, and understand all mysteries, and all knowledge; and though I have all faith, so that I could remove mountains, and have not charity, I am nothing. And though I bestow all my goods to feed *the poor*, and though I give my body to be burned, and have not charity, it profiteth me nothing" (1 Corinthians 13:1-3).

Preaching with love is the "more excellent way" (1 Corinthians 12:31).

Love is a great thing to write about, to talk about, to preach about, but all that means nothing unless there is an example. You cannot dissect love. You cannot exegete love. You have to demonstrate love. 1 Corinthians 13:4-7 gives fifteen verbs describing love. Verbs - not adjectives. The verbs are all present tense verbs, indicating actions and attitudes that become a habit, gradually ingrained by constant repetition.[21]

It is very possible to preach eloquent messages, to understand depths of Scripture truth, to accomplish great works by faith, and even wear oneself out for Christ, and still lack a heart of love. Paul knew it. We would watch his life from a distance and marvel at the love he had for sinners, for saints, for Christ and His church, yet he saw it differently. He had to work at loving people. He had to work at the "more excellent way".

A preacher that loves people "suffereth long." When a church member in Corinth had a case against a brother, they were ready to go to a pagan courtroom, but love says,

"Wait a moment." Suffering long describes a person who has the power to demolish an enemy, yet out of love, he chooses not to do so. It is tempting to listen to the flesh telling us to hammer that rebel from the pulpit, but love slows things down. It is a "more excellent way."

Love is "kind." The Corinthian pot luck dinner became a place of cliques and castes, but the loving man knew no separate tables. If anyone left hungry, it would be that man of love, not the man of poverty. The more excellent preacher is kind to people others don't notice.

Love "envieth not." For the Corinthians, envy and strife were pervasive, but the "more excellent way" is honored when someone else is honored. It is one thing to suffer when another brother suffers, but to rejoice when he gets an honor that I don't get is something entirely different.

Love "vaunteth not itself" - it does not think highly of oneself. A preacher once commented to his wife, "Honey, there are only two great preachers in America." His wife responded, "There is one less than you think."

Love is "not puffed up." Six times in 1 Corinthians the church was charged with being puffed up like a balloon. The pump filling the balloon was the great knowledge the people supposed they had (1 Corinthians 8:1). A "more excellent way" of preaching has no need of reminding the people where a man went to school, or how many degrees he has on the wall.

Love does not behave "unseemly." A preacher that loves his people will never bring disgrace to his Savior, his church, or his family with shameful sin. The word was often used with a sexual overtone, which was apropos for a church that tolerated gross fornication. A preacher who loves people will never flirt, never allow himself to be in a compromising situation. The "more excellent way" sets a standard above reproach.

Love "seeketh not her own." The Corinthians were famous for seeking their own benefit and wishes, yet a preacher of love seeks the profit of others (1 Corinthians 10:33). His life is consumed by the testimony of Christ. "I may have the freedom to engage in certain activities, but what will it do to help or hurt someone else?"

Love is "not easily provoked." A preacher following a "more excellent way" has a long fuse, and it takes a lot to get under his skin. A man that is growing in love will slowly realize that God is giving him victory over anger.

Love thinks "no evil." The word describes a man contemplating and plotting ways to get revenge when he is wronged. Paul's life could have been consumed by thinking evil, as the Corinthian church members regularly misjudged his motives and found fault. The "more excellent way" superseded his personal animosity.

Love rejoices "not in iniquity." A church member was quick to drag a brother into court and delighted when he won the verdict, but a preacher sees that the testimony of Christ in that pagan court lost. There is no joy in sin.

Love "rejoiceth in the truth." It is the common theme that unites a New Testament church - the people rejoice together over the Bible. Sadly, the church in Corinth was divided into its separate camps making it impossible to rejoice together.

Love "beareth all things." The word for all, found four times here, refers to all things all the time. Love has no limits. Love never stops loving. Love never stops bearing (covering the faults of others). Instead of judging people (4:3), the "more excellent way" keeps looking at the blessings and not the mistakes and errors.

Love "believeth all things." It never stops trusting the brethren; it never loses faith. 1 Corinthians 1:10 demonstrates the confidence Paul had for church, believing they would conquer the divisions and strife.

Love "hopeth all things." Paul never lost hope for his brothers. In 2 Corinthians 1:7, he was "stedfast" in his thinking the church would make it to the finish line.

Love "endureth all things." There is a list in 2 Corinthians 11:23-27 that describes the "more excellent way:"

"In labours more abundant, in stripes above measure, in prisons more frequent, in deaths oft. Of the Jews five times received I forty *stripes* save one. Thrice was I beaten with rods, once was I stoned, thrice I suffered shipwreck, a night and a day I have been in the deep; *In* journeyings often, *in* perils of waters, *in* perils of robbers, *in* perils by *mine own* countrymen, *in* perils by the heathen, *in* perils in the city, *in* perils in the wilderness, *in* perils in the sea, *in* perils among false brethren; In weariness and painfulness, in watchings often, in hunger and thirst, in fastings often, in cold and nakedness."

A Jewish woman was fleeing the German Gestapo in France during World War II. On the verge of being caught, she came to the home of a French Huguenot who told her to flee to a new place. The Jewish lady said, "It's no use, they will find me anyway. They are so close behind."

The Christian widow said, "Yes, they will find someone here, but it's time for you to leave. Go with these people to safety. I will take your identification and wait here." The Jewish lady then understood the plan; the Gestapo would find this Christian widow and think she was the fleeing Jew.

This Hebrew lady said, "I asked her why she was doing that and the widow responded, 'It's the least I can do; Christ has already done that and more for me.'" The widow was caught and imprisoned in the Jewish lady's place, allowing time for her to escape.[22]

The compassion of the French woman meant she lost her life, but it led to the conversion of the Jewish woman. It was 1 Corinthians 13 personified. It was the "more excellent way."

Chapter Twenty

Be Understood

"For if the trumpet give an uncertain sound,
who shall prepare himself to the battle?"
1 Corinthians 14:8

THE RESULT OF THE bickering and childishness in the church of Corinth was a self-centered people. Convinced they had a superior brand of Christianity, the elites in the church publicly demonstrated with their 'heavenly language.' Their puffed-up arrogance was the cancer of the church, playing itself out in the very meetings of the church, when they would speak in tongues.

As such, the end game in the church of Corinth was a befuddled people. It was the polar opposite of God's intent for the local church. When a lost man walked into the service, God wanted him to be "convinced of all." He was looking for this response: "so falling down on *his* face he will worship God, and report that God is in you of a truth" (1 Corinthians 14:24-25).

With the backdrop of the Corinthian confusion, the Bible instructs its preachers to prophesy with clear distinction. "For if the trumpet give an uncertain sound, who shall prepare himself to the battle? So likewise ye, except ye utter by the tongue words easy to be understood, how shall it be known what is spoken? for ye shall speak into the air" (1 Corinthians 14:8-9).

The prophet of Bible times was declaring the message that God had revealed to him personally. The prophet of our times declares the completed message that God has given to us all. "We have also a more sure word of prophecy; whereunto ye do well that ye take heed" (2 Peter 1:19). Far better than human thinking is the unchangeable, eternal Word of God.

An old preacher admonished, "Put the cookies on the bottom shelf so everybody can get them." When it comes to preaching, Paul told the Corinthian church that God expected a message delivered that everyone would understand. No one was to leave the building wondering what the preacher said or meant. Instead of their tongues with its bewildering turmoil, God demanded the better choice: "greater *is* he that prophesieth than he that speaketh with tongues, except he interpret, that the church may receive edifying" (1 Corinthians 14:5). In so doing, He left us with a number of lessons about plain preaching.

Our words must be *edifying* words (1 Corinthians 14:3). God's preacher should look at the church as a work in progress, a building on the foundation of Jesus Christ. As such, the preaching is a building block seeking to make a finished product for the glory of Christ. We don't have to preach everything in one morning service. We can save something for the evening service.

A pastor was moving into his second hour when a little guy whispered to his mother, "What is the flag up there with all the stars?" The mother responded, "That flag honors those who died in the service." The fellow asked, "Did they die in the morning service or the evening service?"

Every preacher needs to look at the preaching opportunity as an occasion for building the local church for Christ.

Our words must be *exhorting* words (vcrse 3). Exhorting words are encouraging words. Some are convinced that real preaching hammers the victim until there is nothing left. It is true that a Bible preacher will of necessity preach unpleasant messages against sin, yet we need to remind ourselves of the spiritual beating God's people are taking in these evil days. There is a tremendous need to apply the salve of the Bible to hurting hearts and hurting homes.

Exhorting words are strengthening words. A great illustration of exhortation is 1 Timothy 6:17-19: "Charge them that are rich in this world, that they be not highminded, nor trust in uncertain riches, but in the living God, who giveth us richly all things to enjoy; That they do good, that they be rich in good works, ready to distribute, willing to communicate; Laying up in store for themselves a good foundation against the time to come, that they may lay hold on eternal life." That kind of preaching makes a strong man, a strong businessman, a strong father, a strong husband, and a strong Christian.

Our words must be *comforting* words (verse 3). Similar to the word exhortation, the word means to console a person in time of affliction. Happy is the church member that gets just the right message to meet the need in the midst of turmoil.

Our words must be *profitable* words (verse 6). Reading the book of 1 Corinthians, one easily perceives the sorrow Paul experiences over the spiritual condition of the church. It does not take an expert to understand his disappointment, nor is it hard to find strong responses to their carnality.

Yet, in another sense, every word of 1 Corinthians tells the story of profitable words. Paul is not seeking revenge. He is not creating a bully pulpit to force his thinking down their spiritual throats. Instead, he sincerely seeks words for their profit. He wanted them to read the letter, be convicted over their sinful condition, and change their attitudes and actions.

It is a good thing to leave a service convicted over our sins. It is a better thing to leave a service having repented of our sins. It is the best thing to leave a service knowing how to get victory the next time sin is knocking on the door.

Our words must be *distinct* words (verse 8). Musical instruments like flutes (pipes) and harps have a distinct or separate sound. A glorious symphony fills the hall with wonderful music because those individual instruments collectively do their part.

The beautiful melody of a local church depends on clear sounds of preaching. A trumpeter giving an uncertain sound (a muddled sound) in contrast to a clear, crisp blast will never be able to lead in war. If the local church will move 'like a mighty army' there must be a man of God preaching distinct, clear messages.

Our words must be *easy* words (verse 9). The message must be so simple that a child can get the meaning.

It is a great joy when the preaching of the Bible meets needs in the hearts of people. That work is accomplished when God's man keeps it simple.

Chapter Twenty One
The Gospel!

*"For I delivered unto you...Christ died for our sins...he was buried...
he rose again...according to the scriptures"
1 Corinthians 15:3-4*

THE WORST NFL team in 1958 was the Green Bay Packers. Their record was a paltry 1-10-1. They were last in offense and last in defense. They responded by hiring Vince Lombardi as their next coach.

In 1959, the new coach called for a team meeting. He gathered the players together, held a football in the air, and said:

"Gentlemen, this is a football."

For a moment he looked at the incredulous faces of these professional athletes, then went on:

"As a team last year we were horrible at the fundamentals of the game of football. Nobody here knows how to block and nobody knows how to tackle. What we're going to do now is go back to basics and we're going to learn, drill, and practice the fundamentals until we become better at them than anyone else in the game. If you do this with me, I will make you champions."[23]

Lombardi coached 10 seasons in the NFL winning 5 league championships. In American sports lore, he would join John Wooden as the greatest coaches of all time. He was a winner because he knew how to get back to the basics.

So it was with Paul. As one reads the book of 1 Corinthians, the complex problems that inundated the church threatened to overwhelm them, but when we arrive in 1 Corinthians 15, one can almost see Paul standing in the congregation, holding up the Word of God, and saying:

"Ladies and gentlemen, this is the Bible."

When he had their attention, he would continue:

"Moreover, brethren, I declare unto you the gospel which I preached unto you, which also ye have received, and wherein ye stand; By which also ye are saved, if ye keep in memory what I preached unto you, unless ye have believed in vain. For I delivered unto you first of all that which I also received, how that Christ died for our sins according to the scriptures; And that he was buried, and that he rose again the third day according to the scriptures" (1 Corinthians 15:1-4).

There is a powerful lesson for the preacher of the Bible. We often have a tendency to look for something new and unique. When I hear a preacher say, "I am going to preach something you have never heard before", I usually walk out of the meeting saying, "Yup. I have never heard that before."

Instead of some new thing, Paul told them, "I am now declaring once again the very same message that I have preached in the past." It is a great barometer for a preacher that has been in the pulpit a long time. Do we still preach the message we used to preach? Have we become a little too smart to preach John 3:16? Have we been so worried about finding a new message that we neglect to preach the old one?

This church of Corinth was so proud of their great knowledge, yet it had resulted in a group of unteachable people. They thought of themselves as prophets and spiritual people (14:37) when in truth they were plain, old-fashioned ignorant. By the time he gets to chapter 15, he has to convince these geniuses that Jesus actually did rise from the dead. Like the modern day seminary professor, they were quick to adapt the latest theological arguments in hopes of being found acceptable in the eyes of the modernist philosophers. When one such philosopher, Celsus, argued there could not be any merit to the death of Christ because it was inglorious and shameful when compared to Greco-Roman heroes, the Corinthian compromisers wanted to find the middle ground.

Not Paul. He staked out his ground. He stood for the death, the burial, and the resurrection of Christ. He not only built his ministry on the Gospel message, he trusted his eternal soul to the Gospel message. He reminded them it was the only way to be "saved."

One can almost hear the skeptic ridicule by questioning his authority. "What great philosopher do you quote? What great teacher is your authority?" And Paul simply responded with the words, "According to the Scriptures." He believed in the blood because of the Word of God. He believed in the empty tomb because of the Bible.

Surrounded by the scholarly debating societies of the first century, he may have broken into song:

"Jesus loves me, this I know, for the Bible tells me so."

If we are too smart to preach that message, then we are not as smart as we think we are.

Kate Hankey grew up in a wealthy English home in the mid-1800's. When Jesus saved her, she had a tremendous desire to see souls reached for Christ. She organized and taught Sunday School classes throughout London.

At the age of 30 she was stricken with a serious illness requiring a long period of recovery. Unable to teach, she took her pen and wrote a long poem expressing her desire to bring people to Christ. When it was finally shortened, it became a song we sing yet today:

I love to tell the story of unseen things above,
Of Jesus and His glory, of Jesus and His love.
I love to tell the story because I know 'tis true.
It satisfies my longings as nothing else can do.

I love to tell the story, more wonderful it seems
Than all the golden fancies of all our golden dreams.
I love to tell the story—It did so much for me,
And that is just the reason I tell it now to thee.

I love to tell the story, for those who know it best
Seem hungering and thirsting to hear it like the rest.
And when in scenes of glory I sing the new, new song,
'Twill be the old, old story that I have loved so long.

I love to tell the story! 'Twill be my theme in glory
To tell the old, old story of Jesus and His love.[24]

Paul reminds us well. The world does not need our rhetoric, our reason, our refinement, our realizations, our recommendations, or our religion. It simply needs the old, old story of Jesus and His love.

Chapter Twenty Two
Vain Preaching

"...even so in Christ shall all be made alive"
1 Corinthians 15:22

THE CLOCK WAS rapidly heading towards midnight. John the Baptist had come to the end of the race. From the dungeon known as Fort Machaerus, there came a cry from the depths of his soul. He sent two of his disciples to Jesus with a question:

"Art thou he that should come, or do we look for another?" (Matthew 11:3)

What a sobering thought for a preacher of God - to come to the end of life and wonder if was all a big mistake. We can almost hear John say, "I have given Him my life. I have served Him, promoted Him, exalted Him. I decided I would make Him increase while I decrease. Now I have to know, has my life been wasted?"

Perhaps John was looking for a military leader who would deliver the Jews from the bondage of Rome. He may have been waiting for the glory and victory promised so many times through the Old Testament, and now it was all crumbling. He was in prison waiting his death. Was it all a waste?

Many a preacher of God has struggled through years of ministry. I have been privileged to preach with some powerful servants of God that have spent their lives laboring in obscurity, unknown to most. Week after week they preach the word, faithful in and out of season. Has it all been in vain?

To the Corinthians, Paul laid out this hypothetical case:

"If Christ be not risen, then is our preaching vain, and your faith is also vain. Yea, and we are found false witnesses of God; because we have testified of God that he raised up Christ: whom he raised not up, if so be that the dead rise not. For if the dead rise not, then is not Christ raised: And if Christ be not raised, your faith is vain; ye are yet in your sins" (1 Corinthians 15:14-17).

The empty tomb is everything for a preacher. If Christ be dead, our preaching is hallow and empty. Irrespective of the flowery language and impressive dialogue, a dead Savior means that every message is wasted air. We will have spent our lives preaching a lie; we will die in our lie without Christ. We will then be no different from the religious practitioners around the world who have nothing more than a job to put food on the table and pay the rent. "If in this life only we have hope in Christ, we are of all men most miserable" (1 Corinthians 15:19).

"But now is Christ risen from the dead" (1 Corinthians 15:20)! When a man of God stands in God's pulpit to preach God's Word, he must stand on resurrection ground. His message ought to be full of life because His Savior is the "resurrection, and the life" (John 11:25). There is no room for dead oration and dry sermons, because there is nothing lifeless about the empty tomb. One preacher's sermon went so long that, at length, a restless little girl looked up at her mom and whispered, "Is it going into overtime?" The mother hissed back, "Yes, and if you don't sit still, it'll be sudden death!"[25]

How can we preach without excitement? How can we preach in a monotone? How can we preach without some fire in our soul? After all, the tomb is still empty!

It was Easter morning in 1932. As Pastor Alfred Ackley was preparing to go to his California church for the morning services, he was listening to his radio. The networks were broadcasting the Easter address of the notorious liberal minister, Harry Emerson Fosdick, pastor of the Riverside Church of New York City.

The false prophet said, "You know, folks, it really doesn't make any difference to me if Christ be risen or not. As far as I am concerned His body could be as dust in some Palestinian tomb. The main thing is, His truth goes marching on."

Pastor Ackley cried out, "It's a lie!" He nearly cut himself with his razor as his wife asked him what he was shouting about. "Didn't you hear what that good-for-nothing preacher said? He said it didn't matter whether Christ be risen or not!"

That morning, he preached the risen Christ with unusual power. During the evening service, he gave them the second barrel, but when he got home, he still had not unloaded his burden. His wife said, "Listen here, Alfred, it's time you did that which you can do best. Why don't you write a song about it and maybe you'll feel better."

Alfred Ackley went into his office, read the resurrection account in Mark 16, and began to meditate on the risen Savior. The passion filled his heart until it seemed to explode through his pen. It wasn't long before the lines had fallen into place, and when he sat at his piano, the music flowed as easily as the words did.[26]

Harry Fosdick may have delivered a false message that lasted for an hour, but Alfred Ackley wrote a song for the ages:

I serve a risen Saviour, He's in the world today;
I know that He is living, whatever men may say;
I see His hand of mercy, I hear His voice of cheer,
And just the time I need Him, He's always near.

In all the world around me, I see His loving care,
And tho my heart grows weary, I never will despair;
I know that He is leading thro' all the stormy blast,
The day of His appearing will come at last.

Rejoice, rejoice, O Christian, Lift up your voice and sing
Eternal hallelujahs to Jesus Christ the King!
The hope of all who seek Him, the help of all who find,
None other is so loving, so good and kind.

He lives, He lives, Christ Jesus lives today!
He walks with me and He talks with me along life's narrow way.

He lives, He live, salvation to impart!
You ask me how I know He lives: He lives within my heart.

An empty tomb means there are no excuses for vain preaching!

Chapter Twenty Three
Always Abounding

"...be ye stedfast, unmoveable, always abounding in the work of the Lord,
forasmuch as ye know that your labour is not in vain in the Lord."
1 Corinthians 15:58

IT IS EASY for preachers to get wrapped up in the temporary and forget the big picture. The brothers in Corinth faced the false teachers, the divisive spirit, the rampant carnality, and a host of very real battles. How tempted they must have been to simply throw in the towel.

Paul encourages them with these words: "Therefore, my beloved brethren, be ye stedfast, unmoveable, always abounding in the work of the Lord, forasmuch as ye know that your labour is not in vain in the Lord" (1 Corinthians 15:58). One would not have to be a cynic to ask how this might be possible. The issues raised in these sixteen chapters are more than enough for a preacher to wonder if he just shouldn't quit.

These are truly dark days for God's people. We watch the evening news and see our homes assaulted, the wicked exalted, and Satan winning everywhere. The discouragement level of Bible preachers is at an all time high, with no relief in sight. It seems in regard to verse 58 that the opposite is true. Many have invested their lives in the work of God only to see a church fall apart, to see people they love stab them in the back, to see a lifetime of work go up in smoke. It seems all too often that our labor is in vain.

Then, we turn our eyes on Jesus. We look in his wonderful face. And we are quickly reminded that all of the hard work and all of the effort is not shallow and empty. When we turn our hearts toward Him, He reminds us:

It is almost over.

"Behold, I shew you a mystery; We shall not all sleep, but we shall all be changed, In a moment, in the twinkling of an eye, at the last trump: for the trumpet shall sound, and the dead shall be raised incorruptible, and we shall be changed. For this corruptible must put on incorruption, and this mortal must put on immortality" (1 Corinthians 15:51-53).

He is coming in a *moment*. The New Testament word for moment gives us the English word 'atom'. In Paul's day, the word was used to describe the smallest conceivable instant of time, a powerful reminder that there is a moment of time known by the Father (but not by Harold Camping) when the Son is coming to take the weary preacher home.

He is coming *quickly.* The phrase is "the twinkling of an eye". Allegedly, there was a study done to figure out how fast that truly is:

"For you to see someone's eyes twinkle, light must travel through the front of their eye, be reflected off their retina, and then exit their eye. Assuming that you are standing close to that person so the transmission time from eyeball-to-eyeball can be regarded as instantaneous, and that a person's eyeball is 2.5 cm in diameter, the light would have to travel a distance of 5cm (or $1/20,000^{th}$ or $2x10^{-4}$ of a kilometer). Since the speed of light is 300,000 (or $3x10^5$) km/sec, this means it would take $1/6$ x 10^{-9} seconds...or $1/6,000,000,000th$ ($1/6$ billionth) of a second to make a person's eyeball twinkle."[27]

He is coming *powerfully*. "The trumpet shall sound," and we are going home. When the trumpet sounds in the Bible, it usually signifies the presence of God. "Blow ye the trumpet in Zion, and sound an alarm in my holy mountain: let all the inhabitants of the land tremble: for the day of the LORD cometh, for *it is* nigh at hand" (Joel 2:1). It is a time of rejoicing and glory, for when the trumpet sounds, "... the dead in Christ shall rise first: Then we which are alive *and* remain shall be caught up together with them in the clouds, to meet the Lord in the air: and so shall we ever be with the Lord" (1 Thessalonians 4:16-17).

In other words, when Sunday morning comes (if Sunday morning comes), preach like it is your last message.

It just might be!

An aged missionary couple returned to the United States after a lifetime serving the Lord in Africa. They thought of it as a glorious homecoming. On the same ship, Teddy Roosevelt was returning from a six-week expedition. When the ship docked at the New York

Harbor, the President was greeted by a large crowd, a marching band, and a ticker tape parade.

The husband complained that this was not fair. The parade should have been for them rather than some politician. Even after they settled in their small hotel room, he continued to complain. Finally, his wife said, "I'm going out for a little while. While I'm gone, I want you to talk to the Lord about your attitude."

When she returned, she asked her husband if he had done as she said. He assured her he had. "Then what did the Lord say?" she inquired. Her husband replied, "The Lord said, 'My child, don't fret. You're not home yet.'"[28]

May we as preachers be reminded that we are not home yet. And until He comes, we have been put in trust with the glorious Gospel of Christ, a charge to "preach the Word." Be stedfast! Be unmoveable! Be always abounding in the work of the Lord!

So Paul is ready to sign off this first letter to the Corinthian church. In so doing, he leaves the preacher with one word that says it all:

"Maranatha!"

Endnotes

¹ Prior, D. (1985). *The Message of 1 Corinthians: Life in the local Church.* The Bible Speaks Today (11). Leicester, England; Downers Grove, IL: InterVarsity Press.

² Spurgeon, C. H. (1863). *The Metropolitan Tabernacle Pulpit Sermons, Vol. IX* (p. 189). London: Passmore & Alabaster.

³ Smith, Alfred (1981). *Al Smith's Treasury of Hymn Histories*, (p. 141). Greenville, SC: Better Music Publications.

⁴ Garland, D. E. (2003). *1 Corinthians.* Baker Exegetical Commentary on the New Testament (61). Grand Rapids, MI: Baker Academic.

⁵ http://www.uu.edu/centers/rglee/fellows/fall03/merritt.htm

⁶ http://en.wikipedia.org/wiki/Alexamenos_graffito

⁷ From *Encyclopedia of 7700 Illustrations*, P.L. Tan

⁸ AMG Bible Illustrations. 2000. Bible Illustrations Series. Chattanooga: AMG Publishers.

⁹ Moody, D. L. (1899). *Moody's Stories: Being a Second Volume of Anecdotes, Incidents and Illustrations* (53–54). New York; Chicago; Toronto; London; Edinburg: Fleming H. Revell.

¹⁰ McGee, J. V. (1991). *Thru the Bible Commentary: History of Israel (1 and 2 Kings)* (electronic ed., Vol. 13, p. 107). Nashville: Thomas Nelson.

¹¹ Galaxie Software. (2002). *10,000 Sermon Illustrations.* Biblical Studies Press.

¹² Spurgeon, C. H. (1873). *The Metropolitan Tabernacle Pulpit Sermons* (Vol. 19, p. 465). London: Passmore & Alabaster.

¹³ http://www.spurgeon.org/misc/ep04.htm

¹⁴ http://en.wikipedia.org/wiki/Hugh_Latimer

¹⁵ http://ministry127.com/resources/illustration/a-preacher-that-would-not-be-bought

¹⁶ Zodhiates, S. (2000). *The Complete Word Study Dictionary: New Testament.* Chattanooga, TN: AMG Publishers.

[17] . Vol. 2: The International Standard Bible Encyclopedia, Revised. 1979–1988 (G. W. Bromiley, Ed.) (315). Wm. B. Eerdmans.

[18] Garland, D. E. (2003). *1 Corinthians*. Baker Exegetical Commentary on the New Testament (440–441). Grand Rapids, MI: Baker Academic.

[19] http://strengthplanet.com/other/15-surprising-facts-about-world-class-athletes.htm

[20] ^ Stan Isaacs (November 5, 1991). "Bud's Olympiads Are Worth Their Weight in Gold". Newsday. p. 109.

[21] Prior, D. (1985). *The message of 1 Corinthians: Life in the Local Church*. The Bible Speaks Today (229–230). Leicester, England; Downers Grove, IL: InterVarsity Press.

[22] http://ministry127.com/resources/illustration/she-gave-her-life

[23] http://www.producersesource.com/highlight-lower-right/sales-lessons-from-vince-lombardi-mastering-the-fundamentals-of-success%E2%80%A8/

[24] Osbeck, K. W. (1996). *Amazing Grace: 366 Inspiring Hymn Stories for Daily Devotions* (299). Grand Rapids, MI: Kregel Publications.

[25] Morgan, R. J. (2000). *Nelson's Complete Book of Stories, Illustrations, and Quotes* (electronic ed.) (124). Nashville: Thomas Nelson Publishers.

[26] Smith, Alfred (1981). *Al Smith's Treasury of Hymn Histories,* (p. 249). Greenville, SC: Better Music Publications.

[27] http://wiki.answers.com/Q/What_is_the_meaning_of_'twinkling_of_an_eye'

[28] Hobbs, H. H. (1990). *My Favorite Illustrations* (133–134). Nashville, TN: Broadman Press.

Books By Paul Schwanke

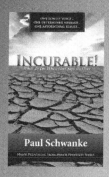

Incurable!

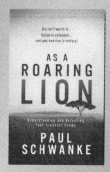

As A Roaring Lion

One Thing

evangelist
Paul Schwanke
1 CORINTHIANS 1:18
www.preachthebible.com

10694245R00072

Made in the USA
Lexington, KY
29 September 2018